RUGS AND CARPETS
OF THE ORIENT

RUGS AND CARPETS
OF THE ORIENT

Nathaniel Harris

Hamlyn
London · New York · Sydney · Toronto

endpapers
Caucasian Kazak carpet with crab
border

title pages
Detail of the carpet illustrated on p.
79

Published by
The Hamlyn Publishing Group Limited
London·New York·Sydney·Toronto
Astronaut House, Feltham, Middlesex, England
© Copyright The Hamlyn Publishing Group Limited 1977

ISBN 0 600 31928 8

Printed in Spain by
Mateu Cromo Artes Graficas SA, Madrid

Contents

Introduction **6**

Definitions **8**

Carpets in History **18**

Signs, Designs and Decorations **34**

Persia **39**

Turkey **60**

The Caucasus and Armenia **74**

Central Asia and Afghanistan **80**

China and Chinese Turkestan **86**

India and Pakistan **90**

Collecting, Caring and Repairing **93**

Acknowledgments **96**

Introduction

Interior of the Mosque of Alaeddin Kaykubad, Konya, Turkey

In the East, carpets and rugs have been widely used and appreciated for many centuries. They have been sent to kings as tributary offerings, and from court to court as highly suitable diplomatic gifts. Oriental connoisseurs have long recognised the finest examples as works of art in their own right, meriting pride of place in the homes of the rich or lucky, where they are arranged and displayed in groupings that have become traditional. And they have also been examined and discussed with the kind of critical attention that Westerners have more commonly devoted to paintings and sculptures. Quite humble homes too have possessed excellent carpets, while millions of Moslem believers have carried prayer rugs with them wherever they have gone.

By contrast, the West remained backward in the making and use of carpets – and in some of the other arts of life – until some time after the end of the Middle Ages. When Oriental carpets did become known in Europe they were extravagantly admired, but above all as gorgeous luxury items that only the richest and most powerful could hope to possess; they were far beyond the means of ordinary people, and were to remain so until very recent times. Though Western manufactories were eventually set up, the carpets they produced were not intended to compete – and could not have competed – with the works of the East. From first to last, Oriental carpets have been more than supreme: they have simply been in a class of their own.

This craft is essentially an expression of Islamic culture, though its history reaches much further back in time; of the non-Islamic Eastern peoples only the Chinese have made carpets of real artistic value. Typical of Islamic arts are a taste for brilliant colours, dense ornamentation and intricate repeating patterns; all these are found on tiles, on pottery, on metalwork – and on carpets and rugs. This outlook is alien to the main Western tradition of picturing the world and nature, telling a story, and conveying 'meaning'; with the result that Islamic art has been little appreciated in the West. Even Indian and Chinese art have seemed easier to understand, and it is only now – with the presentation of exhibitions, television programmes and films – that Islam is attracting general public interest to any great degree.

Though largely the product of a single culture, Oriental carpets offer plenty of variety. As well as austere geometry there is the separate tradition of the Persian carpet, with its splendid hunting scenes and garden designs. There are small prayer rugs made to receive the imprint of believers' knees and foreheads, large luxurious carpets too valuable to lay on the floor, and museum pieces made of silk, gold and silver. And as far as origins are concerned there are rugs made by nomad tribesmen from the Caucasus to

Turkestan; carpets made to traditional patterns, or specially commissioned, or for export, made in private houses or town factories; and magnificent artist-designed works that were made over many years for the Persian court at the height of its splendour.

But perhaps the most satisfying thing about Oriental carpets is that they are part of a living and accessible tradition. Unlike so many crafts, carpet-making in the East has not succumbed to competition from factories; and though mistakes have been made it has survived without being debased by imitation of mass-production techniques or Western styles. The Oriental craftsman works at a loom much the same as his forefathers', weaving and knotting the carpet pile by hand and for the most part re-creating ancient or traditional designs. As a result, every year many new items reach the West which no collector need be ashamed to own; and yet prices are still not impossibly high. This state of affairs may not last much longer, but for the time being at least, collecting Oriental carpets need not be only a rich man's hobby. It is open to any reader to make the natural progression from admiration to informed appreciation–and on to acquisition.

Camel with camel rug in front of the Pyramids, Egypt

Definitions

The distinction made between carpets and rugs is a useful one, but it is by no means precise and carries no special–or specialist–authority. It is simply the distinction made in ordinary speech: between a covering that occupies all or most of the floor area in a room, and one that merely warms or dignifies some part of it such as the hearth or bedside. Both words have been used in this book without too many crises of conscience, with 'carpets' as the general term.

Definitions are rarely water-tight, and this subject is no exception. If the carpet has a single defining feature it is the pile–that is, the tight field of small strands rising up out of the woven base into which they have been tied. Nonetheless there are some objects with a pile–such as bags–that nobody would dream of calling carpets. Probably the most satisfactory of simple definitions is that a carpet is a woven fabric with a pile which is, or could be, used as a floor covering. The qualification at the end is necessary since carpets have at various times been hung on walls and balconies, used to cover tombs and tables, and even draped over chairs. As a matter of fact the restriction of the word 'carpet' to floor coverings is a product of the machine age and goes back less than a century.

Rug-making almost certainly began among the nomads of Asia, who remain great masters of the art today. Once some of these people had become shepherds, the advantages of using wool for covers as well as for clothes must have been obvious: the flocks provided reliable regular supplies, so that the shepherd could keep warm without the necessity of slaughtering the animals for their skins or becoming dependent on the fortunes of the hunt. Later, the addition of a pile gave extra strength and warmth to woven coverings, a refinement which must have proved a boon in the harsh Asiatic winters, when earth floors might be frozen hard. Yet a rug could be rolled

opposite, top
Camel caravan, Iran

opposite, below
Horizontal loom, Afghanistan

below
Bazaar in Istanbul

up neatly and carried without trouble—a vital consideration, given the nomadic way of life. All nomad art is—as it has to be—portable, and therefore small-scale, so that in a nomad context at least one should really always speak of rugs rather than carpets. Finally, all the means for making rugs were at hand and capable of being utilised by the most restless of tribes. Looms for weaving and knotting could be made with little more than two parallel sticks pegged to the ground; wool could be used for both the weaving and the knotting; and there were abundant wild-growing plants that yielded dyestuffs, making it possible to transform the rug's appearance by means of colour and pattern. So it was, and so it still is: the nomadic tribes of Persia, the Caucasus and Central Asia are still employing the same techniques and materials to make age-old designs. They provide a direct link with the earliest history—or rather the prehistory—of the art.

The loom on which the weaving and knotting are done is basically a wooden frame across which yarn can be stretched from beam to beam. The nomad works with the loom flat on the ground in front of him, and does without side supports; the domestic or workshop craftsman sits with the loom upright and facing him. But the working method is essentially the same in both cases. Threads of yarn are stretched from the further (or upper) beam to the nearer (or lower) beam; these are known as warp threads, each of which usually consists of two strands twisted together for extra strength. In ordinary weaving a second set of threads–the weft–is woven in and out across the warp. Weaving becomes the

more complex craft of carpet-making when a vital intermediate stage is added: once the warp threads are in place the craftsman takes fresh wool and ties together pairs of adjacent threads, so creating a row of knots. After he has made one or two such rows, he uses a heavy metal comb to hammer the weft thread down hard on the knots so that they are packed tight; and the knotting and hammering are repeated again and again. The loose ends of the knots constitute the tufts of the carpet pile, which will afterwards be cut smooth and level with a pair of shears. (In establishments of any size this is a job for a specialist, who can often clip the pile to any required length with astonishing

precision.) Edgings that will not unravel (the selvedges) are made by knotting together pairs of warp threads so that they create a fringe at each end of the carpet; the long sides are bound with threads of wool to make firm edges.

The maximum size of the carpet or rug is determined by the kind of loom being used. The nomad, for example, is more or less limited by the distance he can reach forward from a sitting position. Village craftsmen could produce larger pieces with their upright looms: they used to work their way up by adding to the pile of stones on which they sat; but the size of the rug was still restricted by the height of the loom, and, presumably, the knot-

Vertical loom in Anatolia
Turkoman vertical loom

ter's resistance to vertigo. Nowadays looms with rollers are used in most places (though not among nomads), making it possible to create carpets of any length without leaving *terra firma*.

For the sake of simplicity we have so far referred to the yarn as wool, and certainly most nomad rugs have always been made entirely with the one material. But flax and goat- and camelhair have also been incorporated in rugs, and lavish luxury items have frequently been made of silk. Nowadays cotton is generally used for the warp and weft, since it is less prone to stretch than wool. It has occasionally been used in the pile because it gives a purer white than wool, though it has the disadvantage that it tends to become matted.

Many designs for carpets are now recorded – for the benefit of the weavers as well as posterity – as detailed drawings showing the colour of every knot. The nomad, however, still keeps the traditional designs in his (or more likely her) head, from which they are transferred straight on to the loom – with variations and improvisations that are not normally permitted to weavers in more settled circumstances. Large workshops in towns often have design masters who are capable of dictating numbers and colours of knots to several workers at the same time; they too may well keep no paper records of their designs, carrying on the ancient tradition of the craft as a 'mystery' whose practitioners were sworn to secrecy. Such workshops give an impression of frenzied activity, with the knotters' fingers moving at lightning speed to keep up with the master's instructions – and to earn enough to live. Months of work go into every carpet, and it is a sad fact that their still reasonable prices are possible only because the makers are so poorly paid for their skill and labour. The knotters are generally girls, perhaps because they are the

Diagram of knots

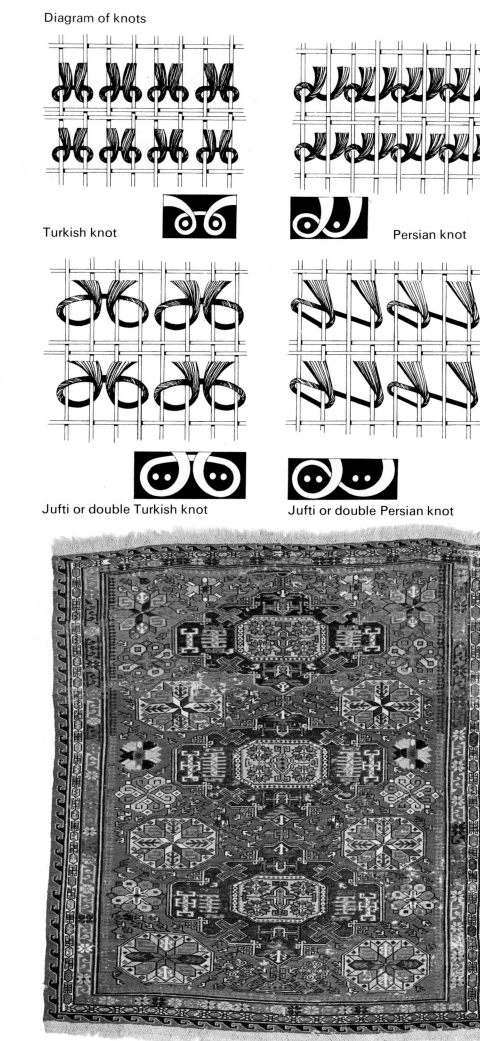

Turkish knot

Persian knot

Jufti or double Turkish knot

Jufti or double Persian knot

Sumak carpet. 19th century. Private collection, Milan

more docile sex in the East; and in practice many have been (and still are) children, who quickly master the manual skills involved, cost less to maintain than adult workers, and are even superior to adults in the dexterous employment of small fingers to tie the finest knots.

A skilled workman can tie something like ten thousand knots in a day. This seems an incredible feat, but a necessary one, for a rug of only moderate size may hold a million or more knots. Exactly how much work is involved will finally depend on the density of the knotting, which varies from one place to the next, according to skill, tradition, demand, the function to be served by the carpet, and the quality of the wool. The finer and denser the knotting, the better the quality of the carpet: the weave is held tightly together, the pile is firm and stands upright, and the numerous and small knots allow the creation of a clearly outlined and very detailed design. Fine knotting also makes it possible to clip the pile very short without the ground-weave showing through; and on a closely clipped pile the design stands out more distinctly. So the ideal luxury carpet should be one that has a high knot-count and is clipped very short. But from the more mundane point of view of keeping warm, large loose knots and a deep pile are far more effective; which is why the rugs that nomads make for their own use have a distinctly shaggy look and rather blurred designs.

The knots themselves are of two main types. The Ghiordes or Turkish knot [12] is carried round two warp threads in such a way that the two ends of the knot come out between the threads. The next pair of warp threads is tied in the same way; and so on. This gives a regular pattern of two ends alternating with two warp threads. By contrast, the Senneh or Persian knot [12] is wound in and out round two warp threads so that a single end alternates with a single thread all the way along the row. Various claims have been advanced for each type of knot, and probably the Turkish is slightly more secure, while the Persian is somewhat better adapted for fine knotting to create a close pile.

The difference is not of much practical significance if the knotting is done by skilled craftsmen. The Turkish knot is used mainly in Turkey itself and in the Caucasus, whereas the Persian is generally preferred in Persia and other parts of the East. There are, however, various exceptions, such as the use of the Turkish knot in Persian centres where the people are descended from the Turkish tribesmen who settled there. At Senneh, the Persian town which gave its name to the knot, carpets are generally made with the rival Turkish/Ghiordes knot—just one of the many examples we shall encounter in which an imp in the inkpot has bedevilled carpet terminology. Other methods of knotting have not found much favour in the East. One that is relatively common, the jufti [12], involves looping the thread round four warp threads, which thereby reduces the number of knots by half: a time- and money-saving device, but one that normally results in inferior carpets on which the pile has to be left long to compensate for the paucity of knots, blurring the design in a way that is unacceptable in work that pretends to any sophistication.

In the teeth of all our definitions, there is one kind of floor covering that has no pile but is generally discussed along with true carpets. This is the kilim, which is made solely by weaving. Designs are created by means of different-coloured weft threads. The weft thread of a particular colour is carried backwards and forwards, but only so far across the carpet as the design dictates for that colour. In other words, the design does not in this case consist of a series of threads stretching unbroken across the carpet. Along any weft line there are as many threads as there are different colour areas—which means that there is a break in the weave whenever two colours

19th-century Shiraz kilim

meet; one of the marks of a really skilful weaver is to minimise these breaks to the point of near-invisibility.

Kilims are made in many parts of Turkey, the Caucasus and Persia; the best and most famous are the work of Kurdish weavers

at Senneh. Since they have no knots, kilims are relatively cheap, and on occasion they have served various humble functions—including regular use as burial shrouds. The famous and beautiful Sumak carpets [12, title pages] represent an elaboration

above
Yarn being dyed

below
Washing and drying carpets in Iran

of the kilim techniques, with concealed full-length weft threads to give them extra strength.

Before the weaving and/or knotting can begin, the yarn has to be prepared in various ways. It is spun, washed and above all dyed. In the East the dyer's craft is an ancient one, with jealously guarded secrets and traditions that have been passed on for generations from father to son. Until less than a century ago, dyes were always made from natural materials–plants, bark, nutshells, berries and occasionally insects. Blue, for example, was made from the leaves of the indigo plant, which is found in Persia as well as in India and other tropical countries; the shade obtained will vary according to the number of times the yarn is immersed in the dyeing vat. Another plant, found in Turkey, yields the woad daubed on themselves by ancient Britons as battledress when confronting Caesar's armies. The most widely used red (shades of brick, sometimes yellow-tinged) came from the crushed roots of the madder, a climbing plant that grows wild over much of the East; and more vivid if less reliable reds could be obtained by crushing the unfortunate female bug of the species *Dactylopius coccus*, giving cochineal. Saffron, turmeric, buckthorn berries and other plants were used for yellows, henna yielded orange (as well as the once fashionable henna rinse) and various berries and leaves were pressed to create greens. Black, brown and grey dyes were made mainly from the shells of nuts and the leaves of nut-trees. Where available, naturally coloured yarns might be preferred to dyes–wool for white, ivory and black, goat-hair for black or grey, camel-hair for various shades of brown.

There is more to making dyes than simply mixing them with boiling water. Each plant has its own properties, and the dyer must know how to prepare it (indigo, for example, is submitted to a complicated fermentation process), and also how to prepare the yarn for contact with it. These are points of chemical knowledge, learned long ago without the help of formulae, by

trial and error. Other aspects of technique include the mixing of colours, and also useful practices such as the addition of curds of sour milk to the dye to achieve lighter shades. Naturally the craftsman settled in a village or town can use more sophisticated techniques than the nomad, and also, thanks to trade, a wider range of colours. The final stage in the dyeing process is to make the colour fast. When the carpet is finished it is immersed in cold water or, better still, hung over a nearby stream which carries away the excess colouring; then the carpet is laid out in the sun to dry.

Carpets drying in the sun

Despite the skill involved in using vegetable dyes, carpets and rugs are quite often streaked or uneven in shading—a phenomenon sufficiently common to have acquired a special name in the trade: abrash [17]. It can occur in a workshop through carelessness or bad luck, as when a skein of wool becomes twisted and packed too tight for the dye to penetrate properly; but it is most often found in nomad rugs, since it is an unavoidable outcome of the nomad's way of life. Moving from place to place, the nomadic dyer may use the same kind of plant to produce a given colour, but variations may nevertheless occur because of the differences in growing conditions (soil, atmosphere, temperature, etc.), in the quality of the water, and perhaps in the texture of the wool used. Similarly, the primitive nature of nomad looms, and the frequent interruptions of the work mean that the shape and design of the rugs may also be irregular. Such defects are not scorned by connoisseurs, who see in them indications of genuineness; and they also feel that abrash and other 'defects' give life and charm to designs whose plain colours and severe geometry might otherwise become tedious. As with pottery or metalwork or furniture, there is something slightly repellent about the perfection of machine-made things.

Synthetic dyes have for a long time had a particularly bad reputation. The first to be produced were aniline dyes in the mid 19th century. These were enormously cheaper and more convenient than natural dyes, but crude and harsh in colouring. When introduced into Persia at the end of the century they had a disastrous effect on the quality of production—so much so that the Shah imposed a ban on their importation. However, modern synthetic dyes give colours fully equal to natural dyes, besides being superior in a number of respects: cheapness, certainty of supply, uniformity of effect, absolute fastness and absence of the chemical ill-effects sometimes found in carpets coloured with natural dyes. Some of these nominal advantages are dis-counted by connoisseurs; as we have seen, they put a positive value on abrash. But the most pleasing quality of vegetable dyes is, paradoxically, their proneness to fading. Synthetic dyes remain true, the colours coming up fresh and bright every time the carpet is cleaned; natural dyes fade with exposure to sunlight and air, taking some time to create the unsurpassed mellow harmonies that have made Oriental carpets universally admired. Not surprisingly, then, natural dyes have never been completely superseded in the East, though there are very few places where they are exclusively used; even most nomad tribes pick up cans of synthetic dyes during their seasonal contacts with town life. The widespread use of synthetic dyes has been favoured by a technique which mimics the fading of naturally dyed material: the reduction bath, a chemical process that tones down the colours without damaging the carpet. Whether even this ingenious pseudo-ageing can give effects rivalling those of natural ageing is open to question.

Old or new, in the finished product most basic elements of Oriental design have remained unchanged since the very earliest known carpet. The first impact is made by the central field, almost always relatively large whether it contains a scene, figures, flowers or an abstract design. Surrounding it like a frame are strips with repeating designs. There are usually three such strips: a single broad one, the main border, with narrow strips—the 'guards'—on either side; but on occasion there have been ten or more borders, sometimes of a cumulative size that dwarfs the 'main' field. As in other art forms, limitation has not proved a disadvantage, and within the limits of this simple arrangement Oriental carpets have evolved in a fascinating and complex way.

An example of 'abrash', or colour variation, in a Shirvan carpet

Carpets in History

Even the most luxurious carpets are made for use, and their fibres will not resist the combined effects of wear and atmosphere for ever. For this reason, almost all surviving examples date from the 16th century or later, and the early history of the craft is largely based on literary descriptions or the details that can be made out in scenes on carvings, in miniature paintings, etc.

From the first, there are many references to Persia (or, as we now call it, Iran), and it is hard to escape the impression that that country has always been the heartland of carpet-making. However, this may merely reflect Persia's political importance in antiquity, which naturally gave rise to more literature than the customs of obscure Central Asian tribesmen. Ancient Greek writers such as Xenophon and Herodotus wrote at some length of the first Persian empire, which twice threatened the liberties of Hellas. The empire was ruled by the Achaemenian dynasty (6th–4th centuries BC), whose founder, Cyrus the Great, is said to have been buried in a tomb covered with splendid carpets.

The Achaemenians went down before Alexander the Great of Macedon, but in the 3rd century AD a new native dynasty, the Sassanids, recreated the Persian Empire in a form powerful enough to threaten the Near Eastern supremacy of Rome her-

The Pazyryk carpet. About 5th century BC. State Hermitage Museum, Leningrad

Centres of carpet production

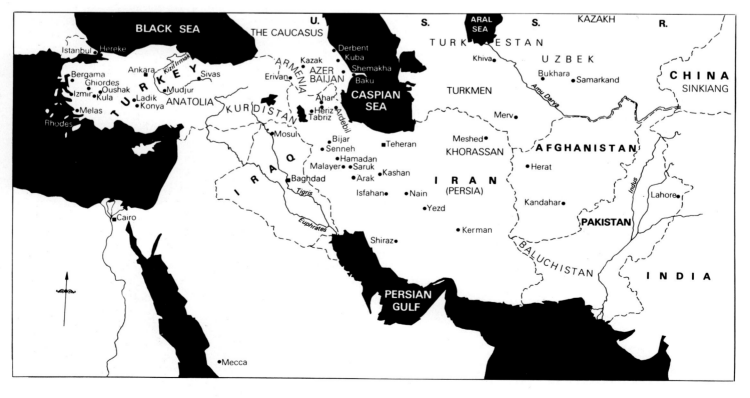

self, which had been unchallenged for centuries. The outstanding member of the Sassanid dynasty, Chosroes II (531–579), reformed the state, defeated the Romans, conquered southern Arabia – and commissioned what must have been the most expensive carpet in history, which was laid in the royal palace at Ctesiphon, the Sassanian capital. According to later Arab sources this was designed with astonishing realism as an enormous garden, with flower beds, stones, trees and streams represented by gold and silver thread, silk and precious stones; the intention was that the king should be able to enter the room and, whatever the season, believe it was springtime. Unfortunately the Arabs who

overthrew the Persian monarchy appreciated the carpet so much that they cut it up to share it out; the pieces were dispersed, and vanished centuries ago.

There are many other references to carpets in early times, notably in Greek literature and the Bible. But the trouble with such unsupported written evidence is that we cannot be sure any of the items mentioned were carpets in our sense of the word; they may just as well have been forms of tapestry or embroidery used as floor coverings. Until recent years, doubts of this sort made it impossible to do more than guess at the antiquity of the knotted carpet. Then, in 1949, an astonishing discovery was made. Soviet archaeologists un-

der the leadership of Professor S. I. Rudenko had spent some time in the Pazyryk valley, in the Altai Mountains near the border between Russia and Outer Mongolia. They were excavating a series of kurgans or burial mounds – impressively large mounds of earth, roofed with stone beneath the earth, in each of which a Scythian chief lay buried. The fifth kurgan had been broken into shortly after its construction in the 3rd century AD, and the robbers had removed the gold ornaments it undoubtedly contained, along with other valuable grave goods. But an accidental by-product of the robbery preserved what was left. Water leaked in through the burgled roof, froze hard and (since the

Mihrab (prayer niche) of the
Masjid-i Jami, Kerman, Iran. 1349

important one, or extremely lucky in acquiring booty. Only the colours are a little disappointing–rusty red-browns, greens and yellows, no doubt much changed from their original freshness as a result of oxydation.

All this indicates that rugs and carpets are of very great antiquity, for the skill and talent shown on the Pazyryk carpet must have been developed over a long period. We should not really be surprised by this, but we have got into the habit of judging peoples by their technology, and half expect ancient or primitive peoples to be 'ignorant savages'; whereas there is no evidence that 20th-century man is any more intelligent, ingenious or skilful than man of the 20th century BC. The Pazyryk carpet, like prehistoric cave paintings, shows that there is change, but no such thing as progress, in the arts. The origin of the carpet, however, remains in dispute. Rudenko believed it was Persian work, which probably came to the Scythian chief as a gift or bribe; and the horsemen on the carpet are certainly very Persian-looking. The other view is that the Persian elements are not surprising in a Scythian carpet, given the contact between the two peoples; at one time or another the Scythians had roamed an area stretching from Siberia to the Crimea, and their relations with the Persians are particularly well documented. So the carpet could just be a tribal product. The balance of expert opinion favours Rudenko, but we are not likely to have a definitive answer unless some new finds are made.

Even older than the Pazyryk carpet was a fragment discovered by Rudenko in another group of Siberian kurgans; and similar fragments have been found in various places, dating from succeeding centuries–in Turkestan, Egypt and Anatolia (modern Turkey). Some of the Anatolian examples were found at Konya and come from carpets made in the 13th century, about the time that Marco Polo was travelling in the East. Marco names Konya first in listing the cities of Anatolia, and says that 'the most beautiful carpets in the world'

stones of the roof acted as insulators) remained deep-frozen for the next 2,400 years. From our point of view the most exciting find was a large (6ft 7in × 6ft) carpet, seriously damaged in only one corner, which lay in one of the side chambers of the tomb.

The Pazyryk carpet [19], as it is generally known, seems to date from the 5th century BC, and is unquestionably a fine piece of work, with a surprisingly complex pattern. The central field consists of twenty-four squares, each carrying a kind of star. These are surrounded by no less than five bands with repeated figures. Two of the guards contain mythical creatures resembling griffins, while the third has stars not unlike those in the central field. More interesting are the row of plodding reindeer on the inner border, their internal organs sketched in as on some prehistoric paintings, and the splendid line of horsemen on the outer main border, some mounted and some walking beside their horses. Technically, too, the carpet is impressive. There are 232 knots to the square inch–a higher number than is found in most hand-knotted carpets produced today. The buried Scythian chief was evidently an

are woven there, apparently by Armenians and Greeks rather than their Turkish conquerors.

Whether or not Marco was right about this, there can be no doubt that Islamic culture had, almost from its beginning, a profound influence on the history of the carpet. In the 7th century AD, fired by the new creed preached by the prophet Mohammed, armies swept out of the Arabian peninsula on an irresistible course of conquest. Persia, apparently at the height of her power, was overrun and converted to Islam, while the East Roman (Byzantine) empire was shorn of the Levant and the whole of North Africa. Within a couple of generations there was an Arab Islamic empire stretching from Spain to India. After a few centuries the empire fragmented and the dominant peoples within Islam were no longer Arabs but converted Turkish tribes from Central Asia—first the Seljuks, who may well have brought the technique of knotting to Anatolia, and later the Ottomans, whose empire lasted down to the First World War.

Through all these changes Islam maintained a considerable degree of cultural unity. As we have seen, intense colours and emphatic patterns are Islamic characteristics, and perhaps features of a Near Eastern outlook even older than Islam. That would certainly explain why the famous ban on representing living creatures, which is not found in the *Koran*, nonetheless stayed in force over much of Islam for centuries. Abstraction, ornament and geometry became the only approved modes of artistic expression, and it is noticeable that even where 'realism' was allowed there was a strong tendency towards stylisation; lettering, for example, was often transformed into superb but quite unreadable decoration.

Large and beautiful carpets must have been made for mosques and palaces at the great centres of the Islamic world; and no doubt wealthy homes were similarly equipped. But the distinctively Islamic rug was one found everywhere and owned by all but the poorest: the prayer rug. The *Koran* instructs the

A Turkish Kayseri prayer rug with a mihrab and mosque lamp

believer to wash, find a clean spot and pray, prostrating himself in the direction of Mecca, five times a day. A rug—a small, portable clean area—is obviously a boon to the conscientious Muslim, and huge numbers have been made for centuries. The ceaseless demand for these prayer rugs must have done much to keep the craft of knotting alive through the Mongol invasions and the other disasters that punctuated Oriental history.

A prayer rug usually carries a representation of a prayer niche or mihrab: every mosque has such a niche [20] on one of its interior walls, indicating the direction in which Mecca lies, and the worshipper usually arranges his rug so that the apex of the niche is pointing towards the holy city. The representation of the niche on a prayer rug may be fairly accurate as to shape, with side columns and a lantern hanging from the apex [21]; or it may be so stylised and fancifully ornamented as to be almost unrecognisable—curved at the top like a head on a pair of shoulders, perhaps [22], or with a multi-arched outline filled with flowers. More devoutly practical objects–prayer beads, combs, jugs of water for washing–are sometimes shown in the part of the central field above the niche, reminding the believer of his religious duties; and in some examples there are even hand- and footprints marking the place he should occupy on the rug. Kilims are sometimes made as prayer rugs, and there are also saphs– long and/or large rugs with a design consisting of a row of niches, appropriately intended for family or group use. Most of the older surviving prayer rugs were made in Anatolia, but there are also Caucasian examples, which are much plainer in design, and a very few from Persia, where cotton mats were more commonly used. One superb 16th-century Persian prayer rug now in the Metropolitan Museum, New York, is densely decorated with verses from the *Koran*, flowers, leaves and writhing arabesques; the mass of lines and abrupt changes of colour create a surrealistic impression of mysterious activity.

In carpet design, as in other arts, Persia is outside the main Islamic tradition. Though conquered and converted, the Persians were not assimilated into Arab culture, and they retained their own language (they use Arabic characters, but write in Iranian). And when Islam was divided by a schism, Persia became the heartland of the minority Sh'ia sect, in opposition to the overwhelming majority of Muslims, who adhered to the Sunni doctrines–a stand which is inevitably interpreted as an assertion of Persian independence. In the arts, an important result was that the Shi'ites rejected the ban on representing living things, so that in Persia, alone of Islamic countries, men and beasts frequently appeared on carpets as part of the decorative scheme or in lively scenes.

The earliest Persian carpets to have survived are the masterpieces of the 16th century, made under the native Safavid dynasty (1501–1722), which drove out the Turkomans and Uzbeks and for the third time made Persia

Persian Safavid prayer rug

right
A miniature from the manuscript of Khivadju Kirmani showing a variety of patterns and motifs in a rich interior. AD 1396. MS. Add. 18113, f. 45v., British Library, London

a mighty empire. The Safavid state was founded by Shah Ismail (1501–24) and maintained by Shah Tahmasp (1524–76); but its climax of glory was reached under Shah Abbas (1584–1627). This Shah transformed Isfahan into a capital of such splendour that the mere remains of its brilliant tiled façades and domes still makes it one of the wonders of the East. Most of the great Safavid carpets must have been made on the orders of the court at Isfahan, either in the city itself or in other important centres such as Tabriz and Kashan.

These carpets are a world away from the nomads' and ordinary town craftsmen's ones, which are relatively small in size and with traditional designs and tolerated irregularities. Special flocks of sheep were raised to supply good-quality wool for the court carpets, and the plants that give dyes were cultivated on state plantations. Well-known artists from Persia and the lands that belonged to her were summoned to design and supervise the manufacture of the carpets, which had to be fit to grace the Shah's palace and also to satisfy a critical and sophisticated audience of courtiers. The carpets were intended not merely to be functional and pleasant, but to be works of art–which is exactly what they are. And in fact a major source for designs was another of the most flourishing Persian arts–the miniature

Persian Ṣafavid carpet with central medallion. Archaeological Museum, Teheran

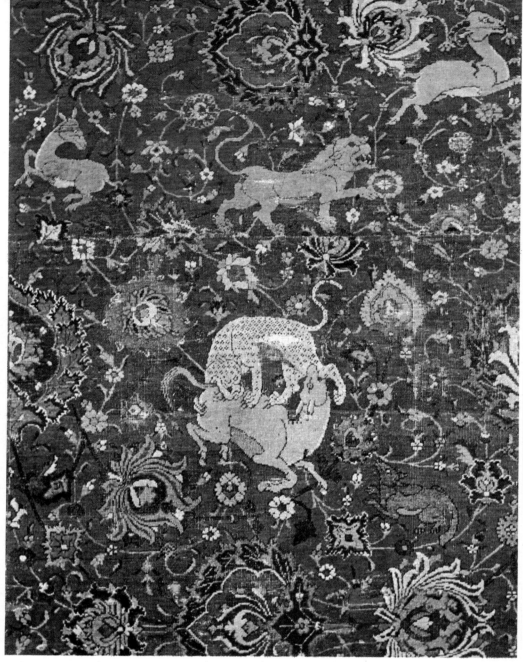

Persian animal carpet. Detail. 16th century. Musée des Arts Décoratifs, Paris

paintings done to illustrate books; and many Ṣafavid carpets were basically 'blow-ups' of contemporary miniatures [23] or individual figures in them, with myths, legends and the great epics of Persian poetry as favourite subjects. This period is one in which the book as a visual work of art was brought to near-perfection, and the superb designs of the bindings are also echoed in carpet patterns. As luxury objects the carpets were often made with the addition of silk, or gold or silver thread. The effect is sumptuous, though to some tastes this is gilding the lily—and slightly spoiling it by introducing an element of virtuoso display. However it is hardly surprising that the Shah and his courtiers ignored such purist considerations, or that they refused to renounce display for the sake of wool's greater durability.

Even in terms of design, Persian carpets are unlike the carpets and rugs of other Islamic countries; the only exception is Mogul India, where carpet-making began in the 16th century in direct imitation of Persian work. This distinctiveness is a matter not just of representing living creatures, but of wider temperament. The general Islamic passion for geometry and straight lines is largely absent from Persian carpets; instead there are a number of types with sinuous curling flowers and tendrils, with or without men, animals or objects. In many carpets a large object—formed from a pattern of tendrils, or in a number of other ways—appears in the centre of the main field; this device, the medallion [24], seems also to have been borrowed from minia-

Large Kurdish garden carpet from Persia. Detail. 18th century

ture painting. The corners of the main field are often filled with quarters of the medallion, and sometimes with unrelated motifs. Cloud bands and other symbols of Chinese origin are frequently used, a fact that indicates Persian receptiveness and also, of course, the wider range of possibilities open to craftsmen working for the court.

Sometimes quite stylised, but still distinctively Persian, are the famous garden carpets [25]. (Some of these may come from the southern Caucasus–but that too was part of Persia until seized by the Russians in the 18th century.) Neatly compartmented like formal gardens or parks, the designs of these carpets usually include flowerbeds, paths, watercourses, populated fishponds and birds. It is tempting to believe that some forgotten tradition or

legend links these garden carpets with the spring garden of Chosroes II. Or can there be such a thing as a national–floral–temperament persisting over a millennium of violent changes?

Animal carpets [24], mostly showing ferocious beasts rending their victims or being hunted down by men, are the most famous of all Safavid carpets. As well as lions, leopards, wolves, boars, antelopes, birds, etc., there are many mythical animals including Chinese dragons and phoenixes. Hunting carpets [26] reflect the passion for the chase– the royal sport *par excellence*–and are often rather gory for modern tastes; the hunters may be decorous mounted archers, but on some carpets horsemen are shown flourishing sabres and hacking into leopards and other creatures. The oldest hunting carpet is in the collection of Milan's Poldi Pezzoli Museum;

the medallion in the central field bears the date AH 929, corresponding to AD 1523 in the Western calendar, and boasts that the carpet is the work of Ghiyas el Din Jami. Despite the date, it is a fully mature work, with marvellously vital figures of horsemen, animals, birds and fish, leaping about convincingly in a network of blossoms and tendrils. Another classic hunting carpet [28] is completely of silk except for silver brocading on some figures. It was made in the 16th century, probably at Kashan, and found its way to Vienna about a hundred and fifty years later, possibly in the form of a present from the Russian Tsar Peter the Great to the Emperor Leopold; it is now in the Österreichisches Museum. Although the figures of huntsmen and animals are again very lively, the outstanding feature of this carpet is the main border, which consists of pairs of mysterious winged

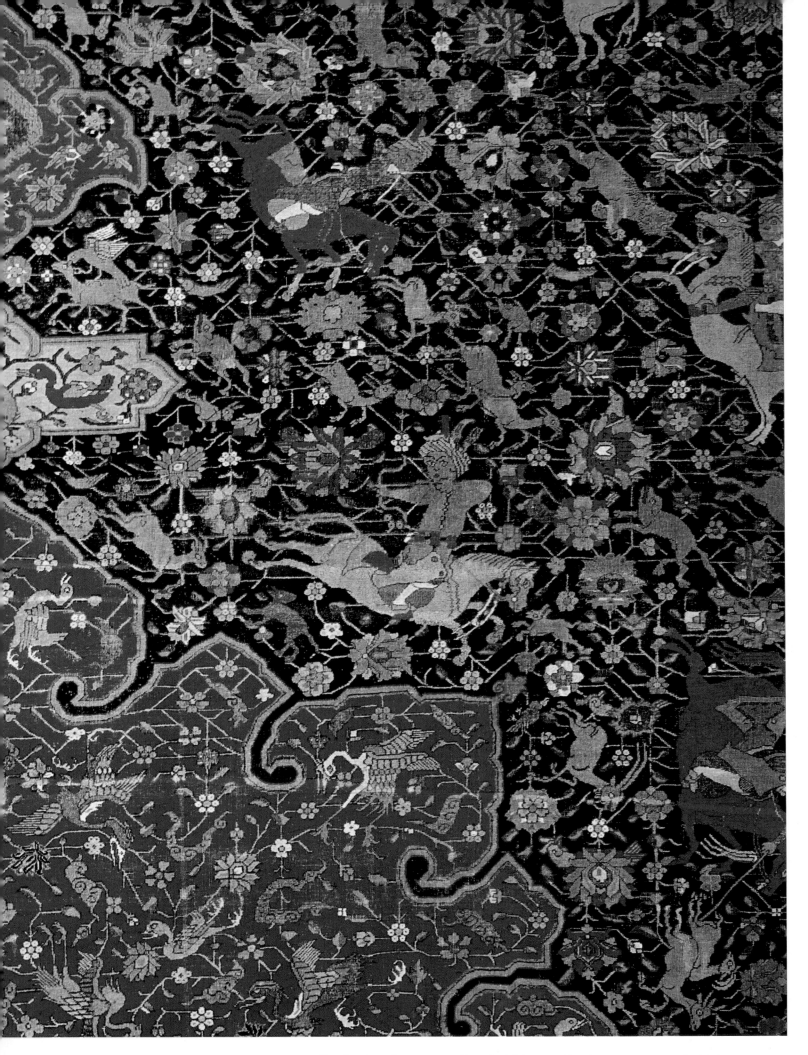

Persian hunting carpet. Detail. 16th century. Poldi Pezzoli Museum, Milan

Persian carpet. Detail. 16th century. Poldi Pezzoli Museum, Milan

Persian hunting carpet. Detail of
border. 16th century.
Österreichisches Museum für
Angewandte Kunst, Vienna

opposite page
The Ardebil carpet. Victoria and
Albert Museum, London

figures, skilfully varied, of whom one is seated cross-legged and apparently eating, while the other serves on his knees. The background of boughs, blossoms, cloud bands and birds is stylised but subtly varied.

The most famous of all historic carpets must be the Ardebil carpet [29] which covered the tomb of Shah Ismail, founder of the Safavid dynasty. At the end of the last century it was brought from the mosque at Ardebil, where the Shah was buried, by representatives of a Manchester firm, and after changing hands again was acquired for £12,500 by the Victoria and Albert Museum in London. Although in a poor state of repair at the time of its original purchase, this very large carpet (38ft × 17ft 8in) was effectively repaired by cannibalising another very similar old carpet from the same mosque. The result is a magnificent object with a superb medallion design; pendants hang from either side of the medallion down the long axis of the carpet; and there are quarter-medallions in each corner of the field, on which a deep blue ground is covered by

subtly patterned tendrils and blossoms. But lovely though it is as a work of art, the Ardebil carpet is almost as notable for its inscription, which gives an exact date—AH 946, i.e. AD 1539/40—and makes it possible to work out how long it took to make the carpet. Since Shah Tahmasp would have ordered it for his father's tomb shortly after Ismail's death in 1524, its maker, Maksud of Kashan, must have been employed on it for about fifteen years. Scholars are still arguing passionately about whether the Ardebil carpet was made in Tabriz or in Kashan, depending on which pieces of evidence—all of it circumstantial—they choose to emphasise.

One other group of Persian carpets that must be mentioned is the 'Polonaise' [30], or Polish, dating from the 16th and 17th centuries. The name 'Polonaise' was bestowed by the French on a collection of these carpets belonging to the Polish Prince Czartoriski, who in 1878 put them on exhibition in Paris. But the belief that they were Polish-made was not confined to Parisians, and seemed justified by the

presence of Polish coats of arms on some specimens. Since there is no doubt that they are in fact Persian, they must have been commissioned by or for the great Polish families. Other Polonaise carpets—of which a fair number have turned up in Europe—were presumably sent as diplomatic gifts. This is made more likely by their extremely luxurious nature; many are woven and knotted with silk, and much use is made of gold and silver brocading. The colour schemes and designs are unusual, and may perhaps have been adapted to European tastes. Lighter colours such as lime and lemon are favoured, and the floral designs are larger and bolder than in other contemporary Persian carpets, with less intricate detail and emphasis on symmetry.

As a court art, carpet-making ended in the early 18th century along with the Safavid dynasty and the subsequent Afghan invasions; Isfahan was sacked, and though Persia recovered quickly, the cultural effects were long-lasting. Safavid designs did, however, reappear towards the end of the century at Tabriz and

'Polonaise' carpet from Isfahan. Early 17th century

Oriental Carpets and the West

Medieval writers were not much given to detailed descriptions of the world about them, so no one can say just when the West had any sustained experience of knotted carpets. They seem to have been made in Spain as early as the 12th century, at first no doubt by the Muslim population, which had been a substantial minority in that country since the Moorish conquest four hundred years earlier. Spanish carpets were sufficiently luxurious to occasion comment in England when Eleanor of Castile arrived with her suite to marry the heir-apparent, Prince Edward. The chronicler Matthew Paris grumpily notes that Spanish habits were utterly alien to the English way of life: in their apartments in the Temple the Spanish visitors hung the walls with silk and tapestry, and, more surprising still, even covered the floors with carpets . . . and were, too, an ill-disciplined lot with an un-

other centres. In the towns and among the nomads of Persia, there was no break in tradition and many fine carpets were made. Local centres increasingly developed distinct characteristics, a form of specialisation that was at least in part a response to Western demand, which by the 19th century had become a major influence on carpet production.

English habit of riding mules more often than horses.

The Crusades must have introduced many Europeans to Oriental carpets, though the record is enigmatic; and, as we have seen, even the observant Marco Polo does no more than generally proclaim the beauty of Anatolian carpets and note that the courtiers at Kublai Khan's palace in Peking had to put on white leather slippers before treading on the Khan's beautiful and elaborate silk carpets. However, the visual record begins at about this time (c. 1300) with Italian paintings which include carpets imported into Europe via Venice

and Genoa, great commercial powers which had no scruples about dealing with the 'heathen Turk'. By the 15th century, painting had acquired real documentary value: van Eyck, Memling and other Flemish artists practised a very precise and detailed realism which makes it possible to identify with some accuracy the Oriental carpets beginning to appear in prosperous households. These prove to have been Turkish carpets with characteristic geometrical designs, many of a kind still made today.

The best-known carpets seen in paintings are 'Holbein car-

The Ambassadors by Hans Holbein the Younger. 1533. National Gallery, London

pets', so called because they appear so often in works by the 16th-century German artist Hans Holbein the Younger. The polygonal decorations and deep red ground of the carpet in *The Ambassadors* [31] are typical, and 'Holbeins' continue to be made at Bergama on the west coast of Turkey. Such undeviating continuity strikes the Western mind, accustomed to bewildering changes of technical and artistic fashion, as both strange and deeply impressive.

North Indian carpet bearing the arms of Fremlin. About 1640. Victoria and Albert Museum, London

Not all such carpets were acquired through trade; some must have been commissioned directly. One proof of this is the existence of Turkish and other carpets with European coats of arms [32], notably in 'Lotto' carpets, named after the painter Lorenzo Lotto (*c.* 1480–1556), in whose works such carpets are frequently shown.

As far as the West was concerned, Oriental carpets meant Turkish carpets–down to the 17th century, when Persian carpets began to reach Europe. As early as 1600 an important consignment got as far as the Arctic port of Archangel in Russia before being lost by the English adventurer Sir Anthony Shirley (or Sherley), who had travelled as a self-appointed ambassador to Persia, where Shah Abbas had commissioned him to arrange an anti-Turkish alliance between the Western powers and Persia. However, there were now more frequent contacts between East and West, and the European royal houses soon acquired Persian carpets–as did the great Polish families who must have commissioned the Polonaises. The close relations between Poland and Persia are a historical curiosity, and it is said that Persian weavers were even imported to help start a native carpet industry.

Until the late 17th century carpets were regarded by Europeans as too valuable to put on the floor. In Italy they were often draped over balconies, and elsewhere they were used as table coverings. The Egyptians even produced special cruciform carpets [33] for Western consumption; the central area covered the table top, while the arms of the cross fell neatly round the sides.

In the 17th century too, carpet-making on a fairly large scale started in Europe, notably in France, where Savonnerie carpets were made with some technical advice from specially imported Oriental workmen. When they returned to their homes the workmen took back with them a knowledge of French styles, with the result that Rococo floral patterns–subtly modified to the Oriental taste–were made at some Turkish and Persian centres [33]: an interesting example of artistic double cross-fertilisation.

Later on, of course, European designs were reproduced in a more literal spirit, and intended directly for the Western market. Until the 18th century East and West were able to treat and trade as equals, but from that time onwards the West was dominant in both economic and military power. Oriental carpets–mainly Turkish–had continued to be admired, but it was not until the 19th century that Persian carpets were 'rediscovered'. These were not sumptuous articles for the court, which had ceased to be made after the fall of the Safavids, but the products of Persia's towns, villages and nomadic tribes–and quite fine and colourful enough to excite the newly affluent middle classes of the West. The demand for carpets was such that, in typical 19th-century spirit, European firms moved into Persia and 'organised' her town craftsmen into factories. Whatever this may have done for production, it was an artistic catastrophe, on account both of the lowering of standards involved and of the use of aniline dyes, whose harsh unfading colours were like parodies of the real thing–so much so that they were eventually banned. Good carpets were made even in this dark time, but it was not until the present century that a full-scale revival took place, partly because Western taste and knowledge slowly improved; since the war, West Germany in particular has imported Oriental carpets in great quantities, while at the same time producing most of the important scholarly books on the subject. Though Western idiosyncrasies are still catered for–for example the American preference for deep-pile carpets–traditional designs are widely appreciated. And in the last few years demand from the Orient itself has increased, thanks to the fabulous sums earned by Middle Eastern oil. Whether this or other economic factors will change the nature of carpet production is a question that cannot yet be answered: prophecy has rarely been such a dangerous and doubtful occupation as in the 1970s!

Cruciform table carpet from Cairo.
Museo di Arte Sacra, San Gimignano

Oriental 'Savonnerie' carpet from
Hereke

Signs, Designs and Decorations

In the majority of Oriental carpets, 'pictures' are notably absent; instead there is a great variety of ornamental devices, inscriptions and, especially on Chinese carpets, symbols. Only the dedicated specialist, dealer or collector can hope to acquire a comprehensive knowledge of these, but a basic general outline does make it possible to appreciate and compare carpet designs more effectively, and is therefore offered in this chapter.

Inscriptions

Words are often inscribed, in Arabic characters, on Oriental carpets. They may be verses or tags from the *Koran* (especially, of course, on prayer rugs), or from secular works such as the Persian *Book of Kings* or the *Rubaiyat* of Omar Khayyam. Calligraphy has been one of the great Eastern arts for centuries, and the Oriental feeling for abstract design often converts the script into a species of decoration. The Persian prayer rug in the Metropolitan Museum of Art is a good example of this, with dense calligraphic decoration in the main border and its two guards as well as in the central field.

The maker's name is found on some of the classic Persian carpets made for the Shah or his court, and also occasionally appears on carpets made since—and not necessarily very good carpets at that. One of the most famous of all, the Ardebil carpet, has an inscription boxed in a spe-

cial compartment or cartouche on one edge of the main field [35]. It reads: 'I have no refuge in the world other than Thy threshold: there is no protection for my head other than this doorway. The work of the slave of the threshold of this Holy Place, Maksud of Kashan, in the year 946.'

Where dates occur in the inscription, they of course refer to the Muslim calendar, which starts with the Hegira—the prophet Mohammed's flight from Mecca in the year AD 622. However, converting dates from the Muslim calendar is complicated by the fact that it consists of lunar years, which are shorter than their Western equivalents. So it is necessary to start with the Muslim year-number, subtract one-thirty-third from it, and then add to it the 'missing' 622. Thus, in the case of the Ardebil carpet, the calculation is:

$$946 - (946 \times \tfrac{1}{33}) + 622 = 1539.$$

This is worth knowing, since it is fairly easy to identify and transliterate Arabic numerals, as shown in the diagram [35].

Ornaments

The arabesque [35] could be called the basic Islamic ornament, occurring in all the visual arts and also at times obsessively used in the West (in the early 18th century and later in the Art Nouveau period). The arabesque may be described as a stylised forked tendril with sinuously graceful curves. The large medallion commonly placed in the

Detail of the Ardebil carpet (see p. 29) showing the inscription

Arabesque

۱۲۳٤٥٦۷۸۹۰
1 2 3 4 5 6 7 8 9 0

Arabic numerals

35

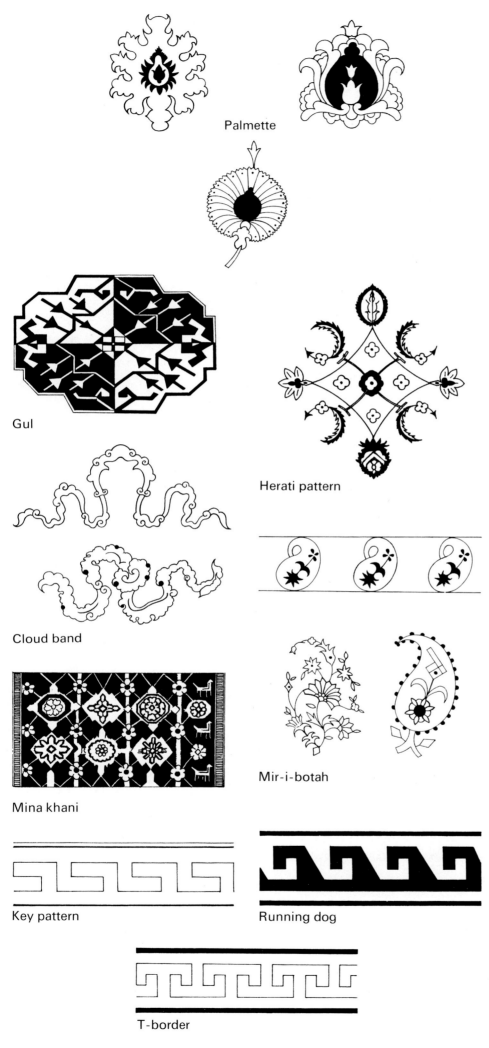

Palmette

Gul

Herati pattern

Cloud band

Mir-i-botah

Mina khani

Key pattern

Running dog

T-border

main field of a carpet is often built up entirely of arabesques.

There are of course innumerable Oriental patterns involving more or less stylised tendrils, shoots and blossoms. Of the last-named, the most important are the palmette and the rosette. The palmette [36] has a central core from which leaves and flowers swirl out (they often look as if they are flapping or waving), except in highly stylised, rigid examples. The rosette is another near-universal device, rendered with various degrees of realism; among the Turkomans of Central Asia it becomes a tablet-shaped polygon–usually with eight sides–and is known as a gul [36]. Perhaps the most famous of rosette patterns is the Herati [36], or Feraghan, consisting of a diamond shape around the rosette; there is a smaller rosette at each point of the diamond, and four long leaves are arranged round it, one close to each of the sides. There are very many variations on this pattern, and in many examples the leaves are so stylised that they look like fish.

The cloud band [36] was originally Chinese but spread over much of Asia–perhaps because of its flexibility. In nomad rugs, for example, it may appear as a more or less geometric shape in an abstract design; whereas on a Persian carpet the cloud band often becomes a writhing squiggle, well adapted to a design with dense tendrils and decorative calligraphy.

A distinctively Near Eastern device is the mir-i-botah [36], or simply botah, which is rarely found outside Persia and the Caucasus. The botah resembles a large inverted comma or tear-drop, and appears as a repeated ground decoration covering the main field, or in combination with other figures on the border. It too may be highly stylised, but no surviving example sheds much light on its origin; it has been variously interpreted as an almond, a leaf, a cone, a cypress, a flame and numerous other objects.

Stars, crosses, polygons and other geometrical forms appear on many carpets but require no special explanation; their antiquity is attested by the design of

36

Persian silk Kum carpet with Tree of Life design

Tree of Life

Comb

the Pazyryk carpet, with its repeated squares and ingenious star-shapes. The diamond (rhomb, lozenge) has perhaps been the most popular, at its most sophisticated in repeated ornaments such as the mina khani [36], with a flower at each corner surrounding another flower in the centre. The swastika, which probably originated as a solar symbol, is a very ancient motif, variously shown facing to the right and to the left. The scroll is another near-universal motif which may be purely geometrical or elaborately floral. On the borders of carpets, variants of the scroll form often occur in the 'running dog' [36] and S-border; and the meander, key pattern [36] and T-border [36] are clearly related forms, making variants on the repeated scroll-swastika-type pattern.

Symbols

Chinese artists seem always to have been obsessed by symbols, a fact that is abundantly clear from Chinese carpet designs. However, carpet production in China has been so relatively isolated, remaining outside the Islamic mainstream, that it seems best to discuss the whole subject–symbols, history, main centres, etc.–in a separate chapter (page 86).

By contrast with the Chinese, Islamic artists have generally tended to move away from symbolism towards pure pattern, just as they have so often moved away from the representational towards increasingly stylised and (from the realistic point of view) unrecognisable forms. Hence the discussions of what the botah is

supposed to represent, or what it is supposed to symbolise: one cannot even be sure which is the proper question. And clearly, discussion of symbolism on this level is not very helpful. Similarly, animals are associated with certain properties or virtues, and there is a 'language of flowers' in the East as there is in the West; but whether, for example, a stylised tortoise on a carpet 'meant' old age in any significant sense is dubious.

Closer to true symbolism is the Tree of Life [37], with its multiple associations—the presence of water in desert lands, the trunk (father) sustaining the branches (children), and so on. Religious applications are obvious, and the Tree of Life is found on many prayer rugs. The combs [37] and water jugs [38] sometimes shown on prayer rugs are reminders rather than symbolic objects, though a five-toothed comb may be said to stand for the five leaders of early Islam, as interpreted by the Shi'ites (Mohammed, his daughter Fatima, her husband Ali, and their sons Hassan and Hussein, whom Shi'ites look on as martyrs and their first two imams). Still more interesting are the prayer rugs, mainly from the Caucasus, in which there is a hand [38] in each corner of the main field above the prayer niche; this is often called the hand of Fatima, and the five outstretched fingers are held to represent the same five religious leaders. Even this dramatic symbol is liable on occasion to be rendered in a stylised form that resembles a gardening fork.

Finally, there is a symbolism of colours. This is generally rather vague and unspecific—turquoise is lucky, yellow stands for riches, etc.—as well as varying from region to region. But one point is worth mentioning. Green is the colour of the Prophet's banner, and therefore sacred; and Sunnis have therefore avoided using the colour in carpets (which are after all intended to be trodden on). The Shi'ites never accepted this prohibition, so the presence of green in an old carpet helps to identify its place of origin. Like many such prohibitions, this one is no longer regarded as valid, so the distinction cannot be applied to modern carpets.

The following six chapters give a region-by-region survey of the main Oriental centres of carpet-making, bringing our coverage down to the present day.

Detail of a prayer rug with jugs

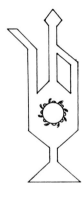

Jug

Hand of Fatima

Persia

Persia has always been a hard land, and despite enormous revenues from oil it remains hard for many of its people. The temperature oscillates between extremes of hot and cold. The Iranian plateau, a shelf of sand and rock surrounded by great mountain ranges and seas, challenges the human will to survive. It is less isolated, however, than its topography suggests, for Persia's position between East and West has put it in the path of every conqueror, and it is uncomfortably close to the Central Asian steppe, out of which poured the Mongols and so many other warlike nomads. Great civilisations arise in response to such challenges, and the periodic revivals of Persia—from the Achaemenids down to modern times—prove the reality of its distinctive culture.

Certain kinds of art can only flourish in stable conditions, and one of these is the carpet—or at least the large carpet of sophisticated design and workmanship, as produced for the Safavid court. That art vanished in the 18th century, and nothing to match it has been produced since then. But Persian sheep throve on soil that would hardly support men, providing a solid material basis for continuity in the towns of Persia and among the nomads—a continuity essentially unbroken down to the present. Nowadays the larger towns are centres of manufacture and also markets to which nomads can bring their wares—and, be it said, there are still several million Persians living as nomads or semi-nomads.

We shall begin this survey in the north-western corner of Persia and move over the country in a roughly west-east direction. The north-west is Persian Azerbaijan, just to the south of the Azerbaijan SSR of the Soviet Union. Not surprisingly, carpets from this area have affinities with the Caucasian rather than the Persian tradition. There is a strong feeling for geometric design (as opposed to the opulent floral designs of most Persian carpets), and though a cotton ground-weave is used in the larger towns many rugs from the villages are still made of wool throughout.

Baksheish, the area stretching from Lake Urmia to Heriz, contains many carpet-making villages, but the city of **Heriz** [41] is much more important both historically and at the present time. The old Heriz carpets were kileis, a long narrow type with soft colours and a high knot-density, especially on the superb items made of silk; they were often very large indeed. For many years production has been geared to the export market, most examples being made with large knots and long piles. Patterns were and are of the floral type, but translated into near-geometry by the exclusive use of straight lines; examples include both medallion designs and 'all-overs' (with a repeat pattern in the main field instead of medallions and corner pieces), most commonly with a rich red ground.

above
Persian carpet. Probably 16th
century. Philadelphia Museum of Art
(J. L. Williams Memorial Collection,
bequest of Mrs M. A. Williams)

opposite
Heriz carpet. Detail. 19th century

The villages of **Gorevan** and **Mehrevan** have a certain historical importance though their current production is inferior; and Gorevan has given its name, as Yoraghan, to a grade of (poor quality) wool. **Ardebil,** famous as the home, but not the place of origin, of the Ardebil carpet, is a village now best-known for stair-carpets, as are nearby **Sarab** and **Meshkin** [42]; the quality of the wool in Sarabs is particularly good.

Further west, still close to the frontier, lies the village of **Karaja.** Here and in surrounding villages the general inspiration was Caucasian, but the rugs carried an unusual medallion design. Instead of one there were three: one in the middle, as usual, with one on either side of it, arranged in a line down the length of the main field; the 'extras' were identical twins, but markedly different in design from the central medallion. Runners and stair-carpets, for which Karaja is also well known, had repeating patterns of three or even more medallions. Recent production has been prolific but of inferior quality.

Just south and west of this area lies the ancient city of **Tabriz** [43], which has a documented history of carpet-making that goes back to the Middle Ages. Tabriz became a thriving commercial centre because of its strategic position on the 'Silk Route', the great caravan route that was the main artery of East-West trade, linking ancient Rome with China and continuing to operate for many centuries despite religious wars and the rise and fall of empires. In the 14th century Tabriz became the capital of the Mongol empire founded by Tamerlane (Timur), and later the capital of the first Safavid Shah. Its shrewd merchants were the first Persians to organise carpet-making into a regular export business, in the mid 19th century. Tabriz is still the third city of Persia (smaller only than Teheran and Isfahan), with about half a million inhabitants and bazaars as crowded and full of haggling over colourful merchandise as at any time in the last few hundred years.

At Tabriz we are already back in the main Persian tradition of floral decoration rendered with graceful sweeping curves; where the craftsmen of Tabriz and Heriz have worked on the same or similar designs, the contrast of results is striking and characteristic. If the Ardebil carpet was made at Tabriz, as many authorities believe, the artistic history of the city is distinguished indeed. Many of the older carpets certainly have medallion and cornerpiece designs, and very large carpets have often been produced: the commercial tradition of Tabriz has favoured the execution of large-scale projects as well as the steady, relatively standardised work of the small craftsman. Men, animals and birds also appeared on the older carpets [43], and some beautiful silk prayer rugs were made. Carpet grounds were red, blue and sometimes white, but the colours tended to be rather dull, partly because sheep in the north-west give a rather coarse wool, but mainly owing to the salt quality of the local water used in the dyeing process.

In the 19th century the adoption of aniline dyes for cheapness, and the long piles left to please Western taste, led to a steep decline in the quality of Tabriz carpets, on which the colours were harsh and the designs blurred. Matters improved in the early 20th century, when a German company set up a factory in which good quality yarn, natural dyes and traditional designs were used. Recent Tabriz production has been heterogeneous. Designs, shapes and sizes to suit all tastes are produced; quality varies, and synthetic dyes are again mainly used, though with skill and discretion. As in the rest of Azerbaijan, the knots are usually Turkish, though the inferior but quick and cheap jufti tempts some makers.

The mountainous west of Persia is the land of the Kurds, a fiercely independent people numbering some five millions. Kurds live not only in Persia but in adjacent regions of Iraq, Turkey and Syria. Many times in their history they have staged long desperate rebellions in an effort to win independence or autonomy. One such rebellion

Meshkin stair-carpet. Late 19th century

ended quite recently, when Kurdish guerrillas who had resisted Iraqi rule were forced to surrender after the Persian border was closed to them. Whether the struggle for their freedom is over for good is a different question.

Rugs are made in **Kurdistan** by both nomads and peasants with geometric patterns or rather crude stylised floral designs. The piles are long, uneven and curly, but the quality of the wool is often superb, and the colours,

always made with natural dyes, glow with a dark rich sheen.

Kurds also form a majority of the craftsmen in the workshops in the two main towns, Bijar and Senneh, where rather more sophisticated carpets are made. Those of **Bijar** [44] and the surrounding villages are quite unmistakeable, being thicker and denser than any others. This effect is produced by the thickness of the yarn, and especially of the weft threads, which have to be battered down against the knots with great physical force to pack in as many as possible. This means that Bijar carpets are extremely stiff and heavy; they have to be handled carefully and are stored by being rolled up, since even large folds would snap the rigid ground-weave. The designs are not particularly distinctive: carpets in almost every Persian style are executed on demand. Grounds tend to be dark, as in the carpet shown here, picking out the vivid floral decoration. Rose patterns in the French style, sometimes called Louis Philippe, were made for export in the 19th century and

have been produced occasionally ever since. The knots are Turkish.

The Turkish knot is also used at **Senneh** [45], which makes it something of a mystery that the town should have given its name to the Persian knot. Senneh—now properly called Sanandaj—is the capital of Kurdistan, but its carpets are quite different from any others produced in the province. Instead of thickness and heaviness, Senneh carpets are characterised by their unusually tight knotting (up to five hundred per inch, especially where the warp is of silk), and by their closely cropped piles, often hardly more than one-eighth of an inch. These features are, of course, complementary, which is why a thin carpet may be at once more expensive and more durable than a supposedly luxurious object which your feet 'sink into up to the ankles', as the cliché has it. Sennehs have a good record for durability, and many experts consider them the best of modern Persian carpets. They take a long time to make and only a few are finished each year, which inevitably makes them expensive. Bold patterns are rare; small botah and Herati decorations have been much used, and so have patterns of small flowers—usually roses—suggested by the classic French designs. If there is a central medallion it is almost always diamond-shaped. The main ground colour is a deep indigo, but pleasant effects are created by the use of light pink, green and yellow.

Senneh is also famous for small kilims, woven so skilfully that the slits between colour areas are minimal, and so carefully finished that it is hard to distinguish the upper surface from the back. The designs are similar to those on Senneh pile carpets.

The output of the **Hamadan** [45] district is enormous. Carpets are manufactured in the city itself, and also in the dozens of little towns and villages in the surrounding area; Hamadan processes and supplies wool on a large scale, and the finished items come back to its bazaars to be sold. High above sea level on the Iranian plateau and at the foot of still higher hills, Hamadan is a very ancient settlement, dating

above
Bijar carpet. 19th century. Private collection, Milan

opposite, left
Senneh carpet. Early 19th century. Victoria and Albert Museum, London

44

back to at least 1100 BC; once upon a time it was Ecbatana, capital of the empire of the Medes, and later it became one of the main cities of ancient Persia. Rugs must have been produced in the area for many centuries; but records are scanty, and most antique examples are not much more than a hundred years old. Their most distinctive feature was the use of different tones of beige-brown from natural wool, usually combined with diamond medallions and/or botah decoration. Modern carpets from Hamadan are of good quality wool but are rather uninspiring. They are loosely knotted–with Turkish knots–and have long piles. The designs are somewhat crude and, surprisingly for such a long-settled area, reminiscent of nomad work: geometricised floral patterns, and occasionally designs with little figures of men, animals and objects, rendered in a completely 'primitive' style. Another curiosity, almost exclusive to Hamadan, is the bar medallion, which is a diamond shape with an arrow emerging from each end on the long axis of the carpet.

Carpets and rugs made in the Hamadan area are generally similar in style and workmanship. At **Ingelas,** just outside the city, good quality wares are made, usually with a Herati pattern on a red ground. **Malayer** rugs are also good, and more varied; here too, many naive little figures are incorporated into the designs. A distinctive type of rug is the **Maslaghan** [47], made only in the little village of Kerdar. It has a large central medallion that is roughly diamond-shaped, but with an edge that has been broken up into serrations; it looks as though it might be an elaboration of the bar medallion. The corner pieces are likewise serrated, and are extended down the long sides so that they meet, creating a most unusual design.

Further south, in the mountains of **Luristan,** live the nomadic Luri tribes, who bring their rugs [46] to market at Hamadan. Their colourful designs are typical of nomad art and are often very effective. The illustration has a rich blue ground with Tree of Life motifs; the cypresses and the whole- and half-weeping-willows, symbolising death and mourning, are neatly schematised, while the smaller trees are reminders that, through children, life goes on.

A Tree of Life, or flowers or shrubs, are often found on rugs made by the **Bakhtiari** [47], who inhabit a large area of the south-west stretching almost as far as Isfahan; the proximity of the city has in fact influenced much of this tribe's recent work, and quite large carpets have been produced. The field of the typical Bakhtiari rug is compartmented into squares or diamonds, each with asymmetrical decorations of trees and other items. Quality varies, but there has been an unmistakeable revival in recent years. The Luri use Turkish knots, the Bakhtiari Persian knots.

When we get to **Saruk** [48] we have arrived in central Persia, where the main tradition of gracefully curling and curving floral designs is dominant. Saruk itself is only a small village, but the older carpets produced there had a very high reputation for their fine knotting and close-clipped piles; the texture was dry, but the carpets were extremely hard-wearing. Most were decorated with rather large medallions and corner pieces, and with neatly outlined floral ornaments. 'Saruk' is also used to describe the better-quality carpets produced in and around the chief city of the area, **Arak** (formerly Sultanabad). This is another of the great carpet-manufacturing regions of Persia. Arak is the entrepôt for many villages and also a carpet-making centre in its own right. Quality throughout the area has been variable for a long time as a result of attempts to cater to Western, and especially American, demand; yet paradoxically it was Western firms that earlier in the century re-established traditional styles and workmanship, with beneficial results that are still seen in the better Arak carpets. Ordinary and inferior-quality wares from the region are known as Mahals and Mushkabads.

Some distance south of Arak is **Lilihan,** which is one of half a dozen villages inhabited by Armenians. These are the descendants of rebels deported from Armenia at the orders of Shah Abbas, who had conquered part of that land from the Turks. Today, more than three and a half centuries later, the villagers are still Armenians and still a separate cultural enclave. They make distinctive carpets with a pink ground and an interesting medallion design which merges into pretty garlands and bouquets of flowers. Unlike other weavers in the Arak area, the Armenians use the Turkish knot.

West and south of Arak is the mountainous region of **Seraband.** All the carpets produced here have a repeated pattern of small botah ornaments, with the 'tail' of the botah pointing in alternate directions row by row. The best examples were known as mir-Serabands [48], with a rather longer pile and more lustrous wool than other Serabands. The ground could be blue, as in the glowing colourful 19th-century mir shown here, with elaborate leafy botahs, though red was more common; cream was also used, very occasionally. Another unusual feature can be seen in the multiple guards around the main border. Modern Serabands are made in a wider range of colours but are extremely variable in quality. The knots are Turkish.

Feraghan is a fertile plain east of Arak, and the name is given to the superb carpets [49] that were once regularly produced by the villages throughout the plain. These were notable for their distinct yet highly detailed designs and attractively subdued colours, which made them favourites in England in the days when a gentleman was known by his taste for restraint combined with

above
Maslaghan carpet

opposite
Luri carpet. Late 19th century

right
Bakhtiari carpet. Late 19th century

luxury. The pile was short and firm, and Persian knots were used. The characteristic decoration of the main field was the Herati pattern, with its rosette, diamond and curling leaves. The pattern was apparently taken up in Feraghan because craftsmen from Herat were resettled there during one of the Persian-Afghan wars. As we should expect, the Herati border—essentially a repeated design of palmettes linked by flowering branches—also became a standard feature of the Feraghan.

The visual effect of Feraghans is particularly pleasing, and often has an 'op art' aspect. This occurs where the Herati pattern has been so arranged that different elements stand out according to the angle and distance at which the carpet is viewed. Even in the photograph shown here, the main field can be seen as a network of large diamonds, a pattern of crosses or, close up, the 'real' Herati. An effect produced by accident is found on the borders of older Feraghans. The ground of the border was a lime green produced by a mixture of

spurge (a plant that yields a milky juice the Persians call 'wolf's milk') and copper sulphate – which gradually eats away the pile. This technical defect produces a result that can be artistically interesting, since it means that the border decorations on old Feraghans stand out in relief.

Modern Feraghans are usually made to less demanding designs, and very few are comparable to 18th- and 19th-century examples.

The small town of **Josheghan** [51] lies close to Feraghan, and there is a family resemblance between many carpets from these two places. Josheghan's great days were the 18th and early 19th centuries, when superb carpets were produced with a vari-

ety of floral patterns and Herati borders. There was a break in the tradition in the later 19th century, but modern Josheghans have tended to be underrated. The characteristic of both old and new is a concentration on diamonds – diamond-shaped medallions, and also flowers and shrubs arranged to form a diamond which is repeated over the whole main field.

Kum [50], about ninety miles south of Teheran, is of some importance as a pilgrim city, since Fatima, the daughter of the prophet Mohammed, is buried there. As a carpet centre, Kum's record is entirely modern and outstandingly successful. Manufacture began only in the 1930s, but Kum carpets soon reached

a world market; the number produced is very large, and sales are maintained by commercial acumen and the willingness of Kum makers to carry out orders for almost any kind of pattern. This of course results in a remarkable variety of borrowed designs in a wide range of colours. In so far as there is any taste specific to Kum, it is for botah and flowervase patterns on white or ivory grounds. The knotting on Kum carpets is always fine, and silk is used in the luxury items.

Nain [50, 51] is a rather similar centre, but production there is more exclusive. The town had an old-established weaving industry which went into decline when its market was captured by

48

far left
Mir-Seraband carpet. Early 19th century

left
Saruk carpet. 19th century. Private collection, Milan

right
Feraghan carpet. Early 19th century

cheaper machine-made Western textiles. The weavers wisely turned to a trade in which machines could not compete with human skills; and when Nain carpets appeared on the market after the First World War, they won immediate recognition. The outstanding feature of these carpets is their knotting, which is extraordinarily fine: a really good Nain may have six hundred or more Persian knots to the square inch. Naturally the piles are very short. Warp and weft are of fine cotton, and the ornaments are often picked out in silk. The dyes too are first class. Nains are luxury carpets, produced in small numbers and only within the means of the rich. Most are now sold in Persia itself or to Arab countries – an interesting reversal of the situation over most of the 19th and 20th centuries, during which good quality work was for export to the West, while the cheap lines were manufactured with the Arab market in mind. Like Kum carpets, Nain wares tend to have light backgrounds; otherwise their designs have no special character distinguishing them from other carpets. Many are 'all-overs' with floral patterns, but medallion designs are also made, as are occasional pieces with animals. Apart from their fine knotting and precise outlines, Nain carpets show a general similarity to work from the looms of nearby Isfahan.

Isfahan [52] was the capital of Persia under Shah Abbas, who moved there from Kazvin, which was more exposed to attack from the Turks and Tartars. In the golden age of the carpet Isfahan held the court workshops which produced many of the finest garden carpets, hunting carpets, and other works resplendent with gold, silver and silk. But carpet-making never recovered from the depredations of the Afghan conquerors in the 1720s, and virtually ceased for two centuries. The craft was revived in Isfahan and the surrounding villages some fifty years ago and quickly reached a high standard. Technically, modern work closely resembles that of Nain carpets, and though the knotting is not quite of fine the knot-count is still high by comparison with most other places. The range of colours is exceptionally wide. The great majority of Isfahans carry floral patterns with or without a medallion; animals, birds, etc. are relatively rare.

Teheran [53], in the north of Persia, has been the capital since the 18th century; since 1925 it has been a great modern city, now with almost three million

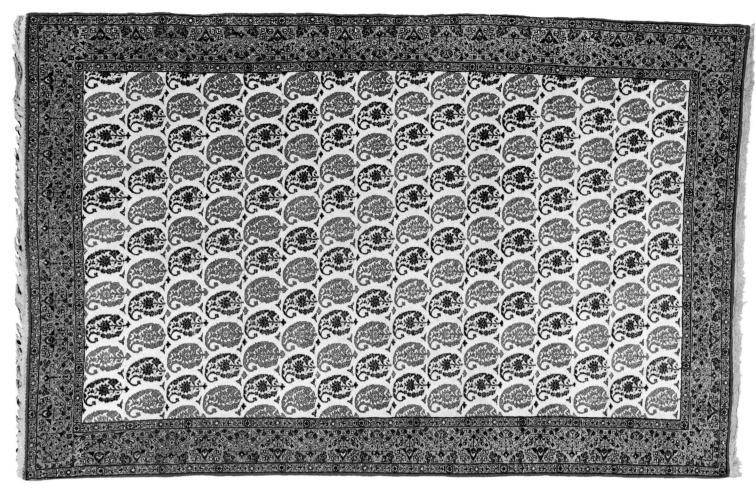

Kum carpet

Nain carpet. 20th century. Private collection, Milan

Josheghan carpet. Early 19th
century

Nain carpet. 20th century

51

inhabitants. Good traditional designs have been reproduced there in modern times, but though technically excellent the work is generally held to lack character. Much more interesting carpets are made in the little village of **Veramin** [53], about thirty-seven miles to the southeast. The design is most commonly an all-over mina-khani pattern with its four-flowered diamond, but flowervases and other patterns are occasionally used. The colours are good though rather dark, but the ground is often a pleasant blue-violet which gains added effect from the sheen of the excellent wool.

Kashan [52, 53] is at the very heart of the central Persian carpet-making region, with Kum, Joshaghan, Isfahan and other towns clustered round it. In reality Kashan is less favoured than the map suggests: its situation, in a small oasis on the very edge of the Dasht-i-Kavir salt desert, exposes its inhabitants to ferocious summer temperatures and unbelievably arid conditions. Yet these unpromising circumstances have given rise to some of the most famous of all carpets. Maksud of Kashan may or may not have knotted the Ardebil carpet in his home town, but the Vienna hunting carpet is almost certainly Kashan work, with a classic pattern of medallion, cornerpieces, and a leafy field through which huntsmen on horseback pursue lions, leopards, wolves and other animals. Despite the collapse of the Safavid tradition in the early 18th century, carpet-making was revived in Kashan in the 19th century with great success, and today Kashan wares—though not quite of the same quality—are still among the best-known of all Oriental carpets. Examples with scenes or animals are usually made throughout of silk (pile as well as ground-weave), though on some only the decorations are

52

top
Isfahan (Teheran) rug

above
Veramin carpet

right
Kashan carpet

picked out in silk. Both silk and wool carpets tend to be traditional in design—medallion patterns with floral field decoration; repeated flowervase or wreath patterns; or, on prayer rugs, a mihrab with a lantern hanging from the apex and two side columns. Woollen Kashan carpets have a warmer, richer look than those made of silk, and the wool used has always been notably soft and lustrous. The Persian knots are fine, but the pile is left fairly long, though it was clipped short until the last few decades. The dominant colours are red, blue and cream.

The road south from Isfahan passes through the village of

Abadeh [54], which has only been a carpet-producer over the last few decades. The commonest design used to be a field of repeated vases of flowers, but Abadeh weavers have also found it profitable to take over the central-diamond design which is a speciality of the Kashkai tribe (see page 54). Ivory, yellow and red are dominant colours; Abadeh knots (Persian) are large, but the finished product is hard-wearing.

A long way further south on the same road, in the province of Fars, we come back into nomad and semi-nomad territory. The capital of Fars, **Shiraz,** has given its name to the carpets produced in the province, though this ancient city is famous for roses and poets rather than weaving and knotting; in fact it is simply the market for the work of tribesmen—or rather tribeswomen—scattered over a very wide area. Geometric or highly stylised floral patterns are the rule, giving the bold simple appearance so typical of nomad rugs. A large single diamond, or a series of diamonds down the long axis, usually dominates the main field, but occasionally the geometricised background decoration includes unsophisticated versions of birds, Trees of Life and similar items. Colours are generally rather dark in tone. Weaving is still so un-industrial that it is almost everywhere done on horizontal looms, and most of the rugs are made entirely of wool. Some tribes use the Turkish knot, others the Persian. The quality of the wool is not completely satisfactory since it wears out rather too quickly, and for this reason 'Shiraz' carpets have never enjoyed a really high reputation. An exception must be

above
Kashkai carpet. Late 19th century

left
Abadeh rug

made for the **Kashkai** tribe, whose rugs [54, 55] are technically excellent and even artistically superior to other Shiraz wares; the wool is good and the dyes from hand-gathered plants.

The **Afshar** tribe were originally inhabitants of the Caucasus. They were deported to the south-west of Persia on the orders of the 16th-century Shah Tahmasp, who was making a determined attempt to subdue the troublesome peoples on Persia's north-west frontier. In the course of this book we have come across several political tragedies of this kind; their only compensation is that they produce cultural cross-fertilisation, and the crafts of Persia in particular are the richer for them. Afshar rugs are produced in a large area between Shiraz and Kerman, and incorporate elements from both—diamond designs from

left
Kashkai carpet

below
Afshar rug with an unusual design

55

Shiraz and the Kashkai, floral patterns from Kerman. The people themselves are part-nomad and part-settled, which makes for a still greater variety of habits and designs; even the knots are sometimes Persian and sometimes Turkish. The rug illustrated here [55] is of an unusual design, with geometric botahs, the tails of each row pointing in opposite directions, divided by a line of small animals.

Kerman [56, 57] stands on the desert tableland of south-east Persia, far from the main caravan routes of past ages. But though virtually unknown to the West, the city had an ancient tradition of carpet-making, and superb examples have survived from the 17th and 18th centuries which include medallion designs, animal carpets and all-over flower patterns. Even in the 19th century the ornaments were picked out with great clarity, and designs of fantastic complexity were executed with complete control. At the end of the century the West discovered Kermans, and European importers moved in to organise production on a larger scale. The skilful design masters and weavers of Kerman quickly assimilated new patterns, both from other parts of Persia (including the inevitable botah) and from the West. Of the ever-increasing variety of Kerman designs the most popular of

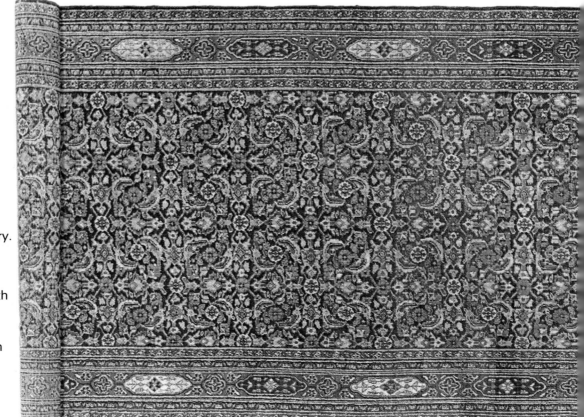

above
Kerman Ravar carpet. 19th century. Private collection, Milan

opposite, top
Kerman animal carpet. Detail. 17th or 18th century

right
Khorassan stair-carpet. Early 19th century

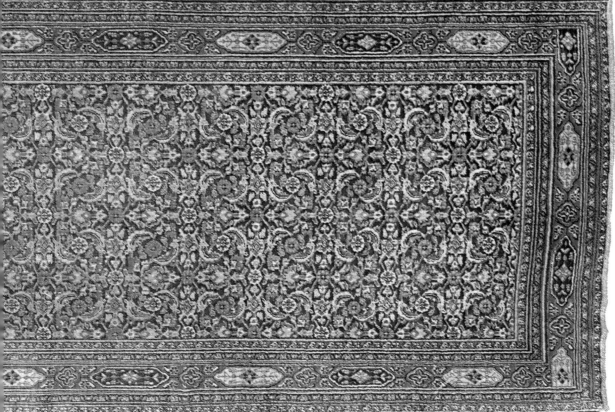

Meshed carpet. 19th century. Private collection, Milan

recent years has been one directly suggested by the French market, with a medallion of roses and a dense floral border that often flows over straight lines into the field, which is a rich plain single colour, most commonly red. Kerman colours are notable for the lightness of their shades. The wool is soft and lustrous, and the Persian knots are fine; the pile was once short but is now medium-deep in deference to Western taste. Carpets are made not only in Kerman itself but also in the surrounding villages; one of these, Ravar [56], produced work so fine that Kerman Laver (a Western garbling of 'Ravar') is used in the trade to describe the very finest Kerman carpets.

Yezd is many miles from Kerman, lying to the north-west on the edge of one of Persia's deserts. But the Yezd carpet industry was set up by weavers imported from Kerman, and the designs have usually been so similar that it is often hard for even an expert to tell a Yezd from a Kerman. Despite this, Kermans have always had a better reputation and com-

manded higher prices: perhaps the proverbial solid reliability of Yezd work has weakened confidence in its artistic value. The carpets we have been discussing are produced for export; but for home consumption the Yezd weavers have long made something unique in Persia.—a cotton-pile carpet. These come in all sizes and are mainly blue and white, with small simple geometric patterns. Being cheap, they are frequently put to use outdoors, whether for picnics or as ceremonial coverings for the courtyard of a mosque.

Khorassan [56] is a vast wild mountainous province covering the whole of north-east Persia. Many of its racially very mixed population are still nomads, and it continues to be an important area for wool production and the manufacture of carpets. The famous Herati pattern (rosette-diamond-four-leaves) is very

much a feature of Khorassan wares, and indeed originates in the province if we extend it to include Herat itself, as it did until recent times. Two interesting features of old Khorassan carpets are the frequent absence of the 'diamond' (actually a pattern of shoots) from the Herati pattern, and the inclusion of not one or two but several narrow guards around the main border.

The capital of Khorassan is **Meshed** [58], a city only a little less populous than Tabriz, with almost half a million inhabitants. It is the most important carpet-making centre in the province as well as the chief market for nomad wares. It owes much of its growth to the fact that it is the holiest city in Persia: Reza, eighth of the imams whom the Shi'ites regard as the spiritual leaders of Islam, is buried in a golden-domed tomb at Meshed, to which huge numbers of pil-

Herat carpet. Detail. 17th century.
Bardini Museum, Florence

grims are drawn every year. Meshed carpets of recent times are usually attractive: the soft wool and mainly natural dyes have been exploited to create a variety of patterns, mainly featuring central medallions on single-colour or flowered grounds. Both Persian and Turkish knots are used in the city's workshops, but the Turkish-knotted carpets (called 'turkbaffs') tend to be the better quality, since the Persian knot employed in Meshed is generally the inferior jufti, knotted round four warp threads instead of two. However, Meshed carpets that do have true Persian knots (called 'taibaffs') are among the finest made in the whole province. **Birjand** in the south of Khorassan is another important centre, also mainly producing carpets with medallions and floral grounds. In the nearby village of **Mud** small close-cropped rugs are made, of such

fine texture that the name of the village has been adopted as the general trade name for best-quality Khorassan wares.

Finally, about a hundred miles beyond the border of modern Persia, there is the city of **Herat** [59] in west Afghanistan. Now insignificant from the point of view of carpet-making – except as a market – Herat was an important centre in the 17th and early 18th centuries, when it was part of Khorassan; and even today the majority of the population are Persian-speaking. The old Herat carpets are rather narrow in proportion to their length. Their clear outlines and accurate symmetry of design indicate the presence of first-rate artists who must have provided detailed cartoons, and also, of course, of skilled craftsmen who turned the cartoons into finely knotted objects with characteristic colours (wine red, deep blue, light

green, shades of yellow and cream) and closely clipped piles. The Herati pattern is first seen on these carpets, as is the Herati border, with its linked palmettes. Both appear at first in strikingly large versions, and indeed Herat carpets are notable for large ornaments, arranged round the middle of the field, which replace the more usual central medallion. As they travelled west, the Herati patterns became tighter and denser and were reduced in size to form repeat patterns that covered the whole field. This may well have been evolved by the craftsmen of Herat itself, who were deported by Nadir Shah when he recaptured the city from the Afghans in 1735. This event, though it by no means decided the issue between Persians and Afghans, ended the importance of Herat as a carpet centre. Modern carpets, woven by Afghans in the large area for which Herat serves as the entrepot, cannot be called Persian work; they are related to the Turkoman carpets of Central Asia, and are described on page 84.

Turkey

13th-century Seljuk carpet from the Mosque of Alaeddin Kaykubad, Konya (see p. 6). Detail of the border showing decoration based on Kufic script. Museum of Turkey and Islamic Art, Istanbul

The Turkish carpet, and the history of Turkey as an Islamic state, begins with the invasion of Asia Minor by the Seljuks in the 11th century AD. Asia Minor was then still part of the Byzantine Empire, which was itself directly descended from the eastern part of the Roman Empire, which had survived the 'barbarian' incursions that brought down Rome itself. The Byzantine capital, just across the Bosphorus in a near-impregnable position on a tongue of land at the very tip of Europe, was Constantinople, the greatest city in Christendom; and much of the Balkans too was under Byzantine control.

The Byzantines had held the line against Islam with fair success for four centuries. However, the Seljuks, a people from Turkish Central Asia and not long enrolled in the ranks of Islam, swept irresistibly over the Middle East and into Asia Minor, rolling back the Byzantines. The fortunes of war swayed backwards and forwards over the next century, and it was only a treacherous attack on Constantinople—by crusaders from the Latin West who were supposedly coming to fight the Seljuks—that effectively destroyed Byzantine prospects of resisting. From the 13th century the Seljuks were masters of all Asia Minor; but across the water Constantinople itself held out.

The Seljuks [60] had probably introduced knotting techniques to Asia Minor several centuries before. We have noticed the 13th- and 14th-century fragments from Konya that have survived, and also the high opinion of the city's carpets expressed by Marco Polo. In the mid 14th century, Ibn Battuta, a North African who travelled all over Islam and journeyed as far as China, was equally enthusiastic. Seljuk work was decorated with stars, diamonds and other geometric ornaments, as we might expect, as well as hooked border patterns which represent an extreme stylisation of Kufic script. But there were also stylised birds and dragons—which were not long to survive the advent of the Ottomans at the end of the 13th century.

The Osmanli or Ottoman Turks arrived in Anatolia when the Seljuks were in decline and the region was divided into rival emirates. Over the next two centuries the Ottomans carved out an enormous empire, overrunning the Balkans, capturing Constantinople after a long siege (1453), and becoming masters of the Middle East, Egypt and Persia. The 15th and 16th centuries were the great age of the Ottomans, when it seemed possible that at any time they might penetrate decisively into Western Europe. They were strong enough to besiege Vienna as late as 1683, but thereafter the tide ran slowly but irrevocably against them. By the 19th century Turkey was 'the Sick Man of Europe', backward and decaying—though it was not until the end of the First World War that the whole structure collapsed and the Turkish Republic emerged as the rump of the old empire.

For most of this period it was the Turkish rather than the Persian carpet that was known and much in demand in the West. 'Holbeins' and 'Lottos' [61] were used on tables and balconies in the 16th century, and though the Persian carpet had a great vogue for a hundred years or so, afterwards its existence was more or less forgotten; Turkish carpets were regarded as supreme until the Western penetration of Persia in the late 19th century caused another re-evaluation.

The Turkish carpet was markedly different from anything comparable produced in the West, and this fact no doubt gave it the added appeal of exoticism. The Ottomans followed strict Sunni practice in allowing no representation of living creatures, including imaginary ones; so the Seljuk practice was abandoned, and decoration on Ottoman carpets was restricted to geometric shapes, stylised flowers and trees, and objects such as prayer niches, lanterns and jugs. Favoured patterns were octagons inside rows of squares such as can be glimpsed on the carpet in Holbein's *Ambassadors* [31], or combined with arabesque forms. The Persian innovation of a central medallion was only occasionally adopted and was frequently modified to make a series of ornaments: something about the single dominating motif was evidently uncongenial to the Turkish temperament. But by the 16th century the range of ornaments already took in scrolls, cloud bands, rosettes, palmettes, etc. The major centre, Oushak, became associated with a stylised bird pattern, and also a curious ornament [61] consisting of three balls arranged in a triangle with two wavy lines above them. There is a picturesque if gory tale that Tamerlane originated the ornament by dipping three

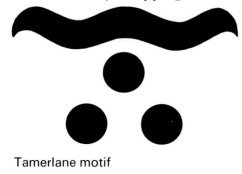

Tamerlane motif

Lorenzo Lotto, *Family Group,* about 1547. National Gallery, London

Transylvanian or Siebenbürgen prayer rug from Asia Minor. 17th–18th centuries. Private collection, Monza

fingers in the blood of a fallen enemy and pressing them against a wall as a seal or signature; but most scholars prefer to derive 'the seal of Tamerlane' from a Chinese ornament.

Prayer rugs became an increasingly important item of Anatolian production, appreciated for their beauty by Europeans as well as used for worship by Muslims. Among the most famous are the so-called **Transylvanian** [61] or Siebenbürger carpets, mostly dating from the 17th century, which came on to the European market via Hungary and Romania in the late 19th century; and once their vogue began, other examples were found in Christian churches and houses. Various stories are told to account for the presence of Muslim objects, most of them undoubtedly from Anatolia, among Christians and in Christian places of worship. But there is really nothing surprising about it in view of the hundreds of years during which the Turks dominated the Balkans, and during which Turkey, however disliked, was the source of luxury and sophistication for the relatively backward Christian populations. Transylvanian carpets in churches are usually decorated with a floral design; by a curious though understandable reversal, it is the rugs for secular use that carry the traditional prayer niche.

In the 18th and 19th centuries new carpet centres developed in Anatolia, though there were signs of an artistic decadence which nonetheless had its points of interest. Floral decoration became ever more important, and on prayer rugs, for example, the niche shrank relatively to the surrounding decoration, while the columns supporting the niche were often transformed into garlands (or, more prosaically, candelabra). As in Persia, foreign styles and foreign demand were influential, though the native tradition never entirely disappeared. In this century, with help from the Turkish government, there has been a considerable revival.

Many of the most important carpet centres are in western Turkey, which has the best soil and climate as well as being close to the Mediterranean network of communications. **Istanbul** itself (the former Constantinople) has no specific tradition of carpet production, though some surviving examples [62] are likely to have been made in the city by individual craftsmen, or by girls in the harem of the Sultan's palace-complex, the Top-Kapi Serai. And of course it was mainly from Istanbul that Turkish carpets were exported to the Balkans and to Central and Eastern Europe in Ottoman times.

Production at **Hereke** [63], on the south side of the Sea of Mar-

mara, was started in 1844. The workshop's most interesting period was in the last quarter of the 19th century, when it worked directly for the Sultan Abdul Hamid, who combined brutal personal dictatorship with a sustained effort to modernise the corrupt backward Turkish state and secure her acceptance and 'respectability' among the great powers. One small aspect of this policy was the production of superb silk and woollen carpets at Hereke, a number of which went to the crowned heads of Europe as diplomatic gifts. However, the work itself was imitative of famous styles, not original; and–perhaps inevitably in the asethetic climate of that time– the styles were Persian more often than native Turkish, though classic Ghiordes designs and some Central Asian rugs were also copied.

By contrast, the **Bergama** area [64, 65] is a historic and distinctive centre of carpet-making: Bergama itself, incidentally, is the ancient Greek Pergamum (Pergamon), one of the great cities of antiquity some two thousand years before the Ottomans arrived in Asia Minor. However, carpets produced at Bergama over the centuries are neither Greek nor Turkish but rather Caucasian in general appearance, with large geometric ornaments and bold rich unshaded colours. The knotting is rather

loose, but the deep glossy pile
and bright colours made Ber-
gamas attractive to Europeans.
As we have seen, these carpets
are identical with the 'Holbeins'
of the 16th century and indicate
that the Bergama style is very
ancient; quite how it came to be
different from that of all other
Turkish centres has never been
convincingly explained.

About fifty miles south of Bergama is Izmir, which in the carpet world still goes by its old
Greek name, **Smyrna** [65].
Though an ancient centre of the
craft, the city became a great
commercial and export centre in
the 19th century, which resulted
in the production of many cheap
inferior wares and imitations of
Persian designs, and eventually

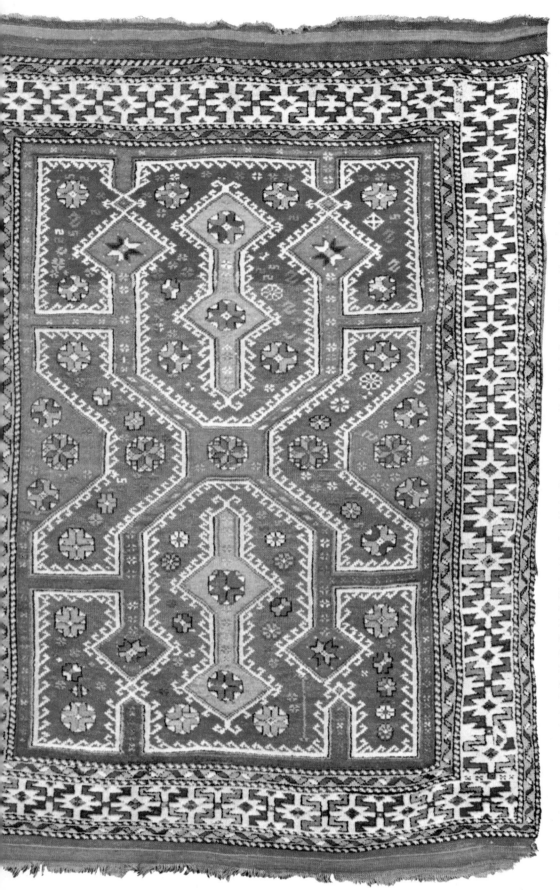

in the manufacture of machine-made carpets. Nearby Isbarta, which Westerners tend to miscall **Sparta,** became closely associated with Smyrna, and in fact 'Smyrna' and 'Sparta' carpets may come from either place. Similar carpets from other centres, with a characteristically long pile to conceal the loose knotting, are also often labelled 'Smyrna'.

With **Melas** [66], situated close to the Mediterranean in south-west Turkey, we come to the first centre of real historical importance. The prayer rugs made here in the 18th and 19th centuries are unlike any other Turkish rugs; in particular, the light colours and large simplified ornaments make a charming impression of the sort we associate with pictures and decorations for very small children. The unusual feature of the colour scheme is the extensive use of a green-tinged yellow; this, in combination with the rather light red of the niche and the white ground of the 'spandrel' or field area above it, gives the Melas rug its immediate impact.

But the design too proves to be unusual. The main field is remarkably narrow and long, with as many as ten borders and guards crowded round it and often occupying two-thirds of the rug's surface; in Melas rugs without a prayer niche, the main field can be virtually non-existent— merely the innermost of a series of Chinese boxes. Even within the field the niche may be unusually small, and like the carnations, Trees of Life and other decorations it is rendered with a feeling for abstraction that makes it almost unrecognisable. This effect is accentuated by the triangular 'bite' into each side of the niche, making the top a near-diamond to which one or more actual diamonds are placed parallel in the ground of the niche. Often attached to the diamonds are octagons with stars inside, or flower ornaments. These interesting carpets are made entirely of wool, usually rather loosely knotted. They are now very rarely seen outside established collections.

In the 18th and 19th centuries, small prayer rugs were made in

above
Bergama carpet. Early 19th century

opposite, top
Bergama carpet. Detail. 18th century. Private collection, Milan

opposite, below
Smyrna carpet. Late 18th century or early 19th century

the nearby village of **Megri** (now Fethiye). These are similar to Melas rugs in technical details, colour and ornamentation, and even in the multiplicity of borders. But a distinctive feature of Megri wares is that often, instead of a prayer niche, the main field is divided into two long strips whose design is similar but by no means identical; several of the triangular 'bites' we have seen on Melas rugs are found down each side of the central stripe of Megris, creating a sort of double linked-lozenge design. Megri rugs are also known as Rhodes rugs, after the famous island, which is only a few miles away.

Ghiordes [66, 67] is the most famous and important of all Turkish centres. The town also gave its name to the Turkish carpet knot, perhaps by association with the somewhat larger and more complicated knot 'unravelled' by Alexander the Great with a stroke of his sword–for Ghiordes is none other than ancient Gordium, capital of Phrygia and home of the Gordian knot. Turkish Ghiordes produced the finest prayer rugs–and almost nothing else–from the 17th to the 19th centuries; modern 'Ghiordes' imitate these classic rugs, but are generally not even from the town itself, which in any case no longer produces wares of much distinction.

We have already encountered on rugs from Melas the disproportion between the size of the borders and that of the main field. It is hardly less pronounced on Ghiordes rugs; but there are other significant differences between the two types. In Ghiordes rugs the prayer niche is often left in a single colour, making an effective contrast with the wealth of ornament all around it. In one example shown here [67], the colour is a brilliant green–a most unusual choice in view of the orthodox (Sunni) Muslim's reluctance to use the colour found on the Prophet's banner.

Other rugs display a lamp hanging from the apex of the niche, or a cluster of flowers which probably represents an elaboration and transformation of the lamp shape. Side columns support the niche in early

above
Ghiordes prayer rug. Late 18th
century.

left
Ghiordes prayer rug.

opposite, top
Melas prayer rug. Private collection,
Varese

opposite, below
Late 18th-century kiz-Ghiordes rug.
Private collection, Paris

examples; later they become flowers or disappear into the patterned edging that outlines the niche. Ornamental panels, or cartouches, above and below the main field are filled with carnations or other flowers, or occasionally with inscriptions. Another common feature, apparently borrowed from Kula rugs, is a series of very narrow border strips with widely spaced floral ornaments, giving an effect suggestive of a row of pipecleaners. Also worth mentioning is the kiz-Ghiordes [66], which is a square, very small rug with relatively simple patterns. 'Kiz' is Turkish for young girl or maiden, and one explanation of the origin of this type is that it was made by girls who wanted to earn money for their dowries. An alternative explanation is that 'kiz'–implying 'not yet full grown'–is an imaginative way of describing the smallness of the rugs. A similar term, kiz-kilim, is applied to the smallest kilims and can also bear both explana-

tions. The most interesting thing about the kiz-Ghiordes is the fact that the arch of the niche, the hanging lamp and related features appear at each end of the main field. This mirror-imagery transforms the field into a symmetrical medallion-like design.

Kula [68] is quite close to Ghiordes, and old prayer rugs from the two towns are often hard to tell apart. The simplest criteria are technical: in Kula rugs the ground-weave is wool instead of cotton, and much softer and therefore more supple than in Ghiordes rugs. The knotting on Kula rugs is generally somewhat looser.

The multiple-stripe border is even more characteristic of Kula than of Ghiordes. The niche designs of the two types are similar, but the central field of a Kula rug is usually not quite so small, and the niche itself, which may have a stepped top, rarely shows much single-colour ground, the spaces being filled in with floral decoration. Side columns and a

central Tree of Life are frequent features. The colour schemes tend to be restrained, with much use of yellow, blue, green and brown.

Even darker are Kula Komarjus. These are luxurious-looking rugs in which blue, black and red predominate, with touches of brighter colour for flower blossoms. The 'cemetery Kula' or mezarlik, is the best-known version of a type occasionally made at one or two other centres. The niche contains a pattern of houses or mosques, cypresses and tombs, usually against a pleasant cherry-red ground. A break in the mihrab outline at its base signifies the believing Muslim's entrance to paradise. Many cemetery rugs were used to cover the tombs of sultans and noble families.

A little farther inland from Ghiordes and Kula is **Oushak** [68, 69, 70]. This is where most of the Turkish rugs that appear in European paintings were made, often carrying the coats

of arms of the buyers. Exports from Oushak continued unabated into the 19th century, when grand hotels were among the most important customers. The classic Oushaks are made of wool throughout and the pile is clipped short, though the knot-count varies.

The first distinctive designs from this centre were an elaboration of the outlines of octagons and other shapes. These were eventually turned into a fascinating pattern of yellow arabesques in a single unbroken line over the whole red field, covering it with lozenge shapes, criss-cross strapwork, etc. The border was an endless chain-like pattern derived from the Kufic script, though later it took on a more floral character, combined with Chinese cloud bands. These rugs are often miscalled 'Holbeins', though there is not one example of an Oushak in the German artist's works; as we have seen, Bergama wares are much closer to the carpets in Holbeins. On the other hand, the Venetian Lorenzo Lotto often showed the rugs we have described in his paintings, so they should take his name–if we must give them Western titles at all.

Another 16th-century innovation was the medallion Oushak, which was probably made with the help of imported Persian workers. (Significantly, Persia

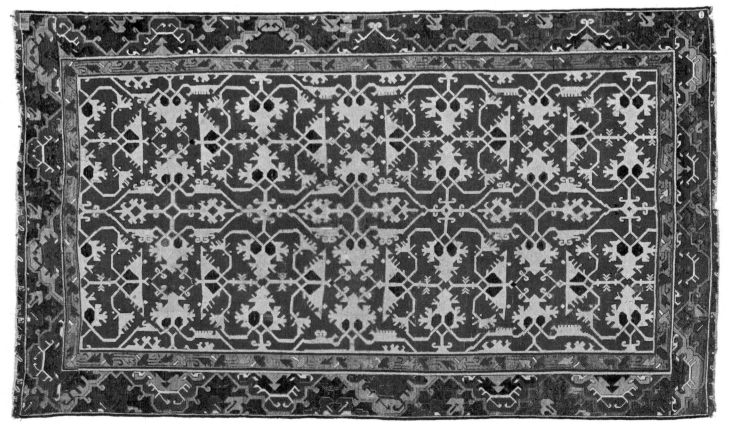

was a newly conquered province of the Ottoman Empire at this time.) However, the Turks rarely adopted the full central medallion design, instead converting the medallion into a row of large ornaments, or creating an asymmetrical design with large floating blue medallions or half-medallions that seem to have been frozen arbitrarily within the frame of a viewfinder. The best-known of the medallion-type carpets is the 'star Oushak', so called because a line of large, vaguely stellar medallions, alternating with smaller decorations, fills the axis of the main field. The colour schemes of all these carpets are bold and simple– basically blue medallions on a red ground, or vice versa. The carpets themselves are larger than most other types, no doubt in response to foreign demand.

Two other types originate from the same period and are often called 'White Oushaks' because

they both have all-over patterns on light grounds, the colour of natural wool. One is the 'bird Oushak' [70], in which rows of bird-like figures and floral devices alternate; the 'birds' are probably geometric shapes that have been fancifully ornamented until a chance resemblance to beak, tail and wings emerged. The other White Oushak is the repeated Tamerlane seal – two wavy lines and three triangles – which is also employed in other centres, though not against a light ground.

Deeper in the heart of Anatolia lies **Ladik** [70, 71, 73], a small town just north of the ancient Seljuk capital, Konya. Ladik is another centre that produced beautiful prayer rugs in earlier times – from at least the late 16th century to the 19th century. On the examples from the early period the niche has not one but three angled arches, the central arch standing somewhat higher than the others. Equally characteristic are the very slender and elegant pillars supporting the arches; in fact this type of rug is often called a 'column Ladik'. The border consists of six-sided lozenges or cartouches carrying floral or arabesque ornament. By the 18th century the vogue for floral deco-

ration, which made an impact on most Turkish carpets, led to the replacement of leaf decoration by a panel above the niche containing a row of stiff-stemmed, very stylised flowers. This can be seen in the early 18th-century rug shown here [71], which is also interesting in that the border lozenges are, so to speak, caught in the act of changing from a geometric to a floral shape: the ornament is now clearly a flower, but its origin in a six-sided shape is still visible.

The most popular flower on early 18th-century rugs, whether from Ladik or from other centres, was the tulip [73]; and its history is interesting enough to justify a short digression. It was from Turkey that the flower had originally been introduced into Holland in the 16th century. When it was re-introduced to Turkey in an improved form at the end of the 17th century, there was a mild Turkish form of the 'tulip mania' which the Dutch had experienced and which Alexandre Dumas describes in *The Black Tulip*. The Sultan Ahmed III had a passion for tulips that was so well known that the period of peace and enlightenment at the end of his reign is called 'the tulip period' (1718–30). Thousands of these flowers were grown in the palace gardens, and during festivities they were lit up by tiny lamps placed in their heads. The appeal of the tulip as decoration must have been enhanced by its clean lines and regular curves: the 'natural' tulip already looks rather stylised before the designer or craftsman gets to work on it.

To return to Ladiks, in the course of the 18th century the triple-arched niche tended to be abandoned in favour of a single-arched but stepped form, like a ziggurat or Central American pyramid. The main field shrank, and the borders multiplied. But most distinctive of all was the large panel inserted below the prayer niche [70]. In this the triple-arched niche reappeared, variously elaborated and decorated with large flower-heads between the arches and dangling from the apexes and the inverted arches created by the links between them. These pendant flowers, sometimes echoed in the

Bird Oushak carpet

left
Ladik prayer rug

main niche, are all that remains of the earlier columns.

In Ladik prayer rugs both ground-weave and pile are generally made of wool. The knotting is fine, and the pile clipped very short. Modern 'Ladiks' are inferior in quality and design.

Ladik rounds off the list of great Turkish centres, though interesting work of a less sophisti-

Ladik prayer rug. Early 18th century

19th-century Sivas carpet with Tree of Life design. Private collection, Milan

producing variations on, the classic Persian carpets. Both all-over floral patterns and medallion designs were used, most often in a style reminiscent of Tabriz carpets. However, Sivas carpets had a lighter range of colours, including pleasant pastel greens and pinks; the ground was often the natural colour of the wool. These carpets were excellent both artistically and technically until the First World War. Later on the quality of work and material suffered as a result of overproduction. At **Kayseri** (Caesarea) to the south-west, similar carpets were produced after the war, with rather better results than Sivas was getting at that time. The colours – rich reds and blues on a light field – were particularly attractive, and the carpets themselves were often of silk.

More original work has been done at two villages, very close to each other, which lie northwest of Kayseri. The rugs of Kirsehir and Mudjur show a strong feeling for geometry which is perhaps natural in the mountainous south-east of Turkey, close to nomad territory. Floral patterns were woven in the area when the influence of French styles was at its height in Turkey, but in most examples the floral element is vestigial. **Kirsehir** has produced 'cemetery' prayer rugs, and also rugs with geometrical designs dominated by large lozenge-shapes. The colours have long been admired, and especially the cherry-red and pastel green. **Mudjur** rugs are very similar, though the colours are noticeably stronger. The niche on Mudjurs is usually filled with a single colour and has a stepped apex. In both Kirsehirs and Mudjurs the apex often culminates in a little crest or cap. Both types of rug are made entirely of wool and have a medium high knot-count.

Finally, there are the nomads of Turkey – the Yuruks in the south-east and the Kurds around the frontiers with Iraq and Persia, which cut them off from their fellow Kurds. **Yuruks** [73] are and have been produced in large numbers. They are often remarkably shaggy, with a very long pile that explains the size and simplicity of their designs; these are, as we should expect, entirely geo-

cated nature has been done in the eastern half of the country. First, however, it is worth mentioning a few more places which have specialised in imitations – and not always despicable ones at that. Earlier in this century **Panderma,** on the Sea of Marmara, produced delightful, finely knotted reproductions of Ghiordes and Kula prayer rugs in a pleasant range of light colours. And not far away, at the old Ottoman capital **Brussa,** the classic designs of both Turkey and Persia were copied, often in finely woven silk. At **Sivas** [72] in eastern Turkey, production was concentrated from the early 19th century on imitating, or

metrical and consist of diamonds, octagons and other basic shapes, enlivened by the frequent use of wavy zigzags. The ground-weave is of wool or goat-hair, whereas the pile is wool. The colours add greatly to the interest of these rugs, with yellow and shades of blue predominating; vegetable dyes were used down to quite recent times. The rugs of the Turkish **Kurds** are less distinctive, having shorter piles and more restrained colour schemes, but they are typical of nomad work. Turkish nomad carpets have often been sold under the name 'Sultans', though for no ascertainable reason other than effective advertisement.

above
Yuruk carpet

Ladik tulip prayer rug. Late 17th century

The Caucasus and Armenia

Modern Erivan carpet with dragon design

17th-century Kuba dragon carpet

The Caucasus and Armenia take up most of the neck of land separating the Black Sea from the Caspian—a substantial neck, about four hundred miles wide. It is mostly wild and rugged country, dominated by great peaks and ravines. The Greater Caucasus Mountains, among which Europe's highest peak, Mount Elbrus, towers to 18,481 feet, run across the land from the north-west to the south-east, broken only by a couple of high passes; and roughly parallel with this chain is the Lesser Caucasus further south.

The position of the Caucasus, adjacent to Turkey, Persia and Russia, has shaped much of its history. All three great powers have ruled it at various times, and the larger units comprising the Caucasus, such as Armenia and Georgia, have enjoyed only brief periods of independence. On the other hand the terrain made it difficult to control closely, and for example Persian rule in the 17th and 18th centuries was exercised very slackly through semi-autonomous khans. Russia drove out both Persians and Turks, and established general control early in the 19th century—though the Muslims of Dagestan, under their legendary leader Shamil, held out until 1859. As a result, the area is today part of the Soviet Union, and consists of several autonomous republics.

Politics and topography have combined to produce an extraordinarily mixed population. The migrations of tribes and the passage of armies left behind those who could not or would not go on; and the Caucasus was a natural place of refuge for the persecuted or defeated. Clinging to the sides of mountains, such groups had little contact with other settlements and so retained their original character, with the result that well over a hundred different languages are spoken in this region: some, like Georgian, by a million people, others by the inhabitants of a few villages.

National and tribal differences are reflected in the carpets made by the Caucasian peoples: they too vary from one place to another, sometimes only a few miles apart. On the other hand there are general similarities that distinguish Caucasian carpets from all others. The knots used are always Turkish, and cotton has only occasionally been used in the ground-weave although it is grown in the region; most Caucasian carpets are made of wool throughout. Designs are almost exclusively geometric, though highly schematised human and animal figures do appear in some areas. Patterns are large and boldly outlined; the colours are bright but plain, lacking any

subtleties of shading. Where these features are most emphatic, the effect is oddly powerful–a clear-cut brilliance that often seems to hint at barbaric drama despite the abstract nature of the design. This bright hard-edged, almost heraldic quality makes it generally speaking very easy to identify a carpet as coming from the Caucasus. Modified in a thousand ways, the designs yet preserve something of their original inspiration–the work of those Turkish tribes who passed through the Caucasus on their way from Central Asia to Anatolia in the 9th and 10th centuries AD. However, the later history of carpet-making in the Caucasus is by no means clear. The stylistic influences–mainly Persian and Turkish–are known, and it is not too difficult to trace their adoption and general absorption into the Caucasian ethos. But it is more difficult to reconcile the scale of manufacture with what is known of the conditions of life in the Caucasus. Nomads and villagers produced small carpets (i.e. rugs) just as we should expect. But a good many carpets have also survived–carpets, that is, in the more restricted sense of the word: some are up to twenty feet long. This is beyond the capacity of nomad and village looms, and implies well-organised workshops, whose owners could finance themselves and their employees over the long periods that it would take to produce such large carpets.

above left
Kazak carpet

Kazak 'eagle' carpet. 19th century.
Private collection, Varese

Taken in combination with the appearance of what seem to be Caucasian carpets in 15th-century painting, this is a tempting subject for speculation. It is still possible that accident or research will reveal some surprising facts about the history of the Caucasus.

The **Armenians,** like the Kurds, are a people unwillingly spread over several frontiers; and as traders and craftsmen, long habituated to town life, they have penetrated places some distance from their divided homeland. A type of 16th- and 17th-century carpet, the dragon carpet [74], seems to have been made in Armenia and marketed at Kuba, far away on the Caspian side of the Caucasus, where there was a large Armenian merchant community, which is why these carpets were long attri-

buted to Kuba itself. The carpets are very long and narrow. Their chief feature is the presence of dragons, or repeated motifs of a dragon and phoenix in combat, which are Chinese in origin and can also be seen on some very old Turkish carpets. In the 16th-century examples the animals are elongated and brilliantly patterned, and often alternate with large palmettes; but they are, unmistakeably, animals. Later they take on an increasingly floral-geometric character, the jagged outlines of the beasts formalising into shapes that look more like leaf-edges; locked in combat, dragon and phoenix come to resemble a leaf or polygon. But at all stages of its development this is a very elegant carpet with splendid patterns and colours. Today carpets are still made in Soviet Armenia, with production centred on the capital Erivan; but the wares are no longer of separate interest, being mainly in the style of good-quality Shirvan carpets.

The district of **Karabagh** is also mainly populated by Armenians, but its position on the frontier with Persia has made it susceptible to influence from the older and greater culture. At some time or other, the best-known Persian designs have been followed in Karabagh – medallions, botahs, Heratis – often rather larger than their Persian equivalents. But Karabagh carpets are almost always long and narrow, and there are other features that make it possible to identify them. Warp and weft, as well as the pile, are made of wool; the knots are Turkish; and the colour scheme is one of striking contrast between the dark ground colours and the brightness of the patterns and ornaments. One unusual colour is a purple-red, much deeper than madder-red, which is a form of cochineal obtained from a local insect species. The finest Karabaghs generally come from the chief city in the area, Shusha.

Another influence on Karabagh carpets has been French. From the 18th century onwards, Savonnerie floral designs were imitated, with a degree of stylisation that no doubt results from temperamental outlook as well as limits of expertise. In the example shown here [77], the contrast between the dark ground and the large soft bright simplified flowers is extremely effective; notice the intrusion of diamonds, stars, stylised animal figures, etc. Comparison with a typical carpet from the Savonnerie factory itself illuminates some of the differences between East and West.

North and north-west of these Armenian areas live the **Kazaks,** many of whom are still semi-nomadic shepherds. Almost all of their works consist of rugs – sometimes quite long, but never wide enough to describe as a full-size carpet – with a long thick glossy pile, the like of which is rarely found elsewhere in the Caucasus. Furthermore, the whole approach to design on Kazak rugs is quite individual, so that the end-products, however varied,

are unmistakeable. Instead of dense intricate decoration, there is an air of largeness about Kazak rugs, created either by spacing out decorations on a plain-colour ground, or by filling virtually the whole field with a few unusually large ornaments. The more spacious of the two approaches can be seen on the superb rug [75] with the polygonal medallion, the complexity of the shape-within-the-shape of the medallion being set off by the rectangle of the brown and white border. The rug is also a good example of the colour contrasts employed by the Kazaks, which are often audacious, sometimes jarring – and sometimes, as here, triumphantly successful.

Somewhat more complex designs are created by rows of octagonal or diamond-shaped medallions, but the *pièce de résistance* of Kazak designs is the 'eagle' [75], which most com-

pletely embodies that people's predilection for jagged edges, hooks and points. The 'eagle' is the space-filler: two – sometimes more on the longer rugs – dominate the whole main field, as in the illustration, crowding out everything but a few little rosettes and jigsaw pieces; the areas of flat colour are here mostly inside the 'medallion', leaving a relatively small area of ground. There is something irresistibly exciting and forceful about this design, with its dramatically outflung blades or limbs. The associations it suggests are powerful. One is the eagle of heraldry – perhaps the rapacious double-headed eagle found on the banners of the old German and Russian empires; another is some sinister multiple-bladed weapon or tool. In spite of this, it is quite possible that the 'eagle' is simply a stylised, much elaborated floral ornament; or that the

'blades' are an exaggerated version of the stepped sides characteristic of the Caucasus.

Kazak borders also show a taste for spiky figures: running dogs, arrowheads and, most notably, series of crab-like objects [end papers]–stylised, possibly floral in origin, yet often apparently in procession round the edge of the rug.

Dagestan, 'the land of mountains', is probably the wildest part of the wild Caucasus, a landscape seemingly torn out of living rock and yet in parts offering rich pasture to flocks and shepherds. Very old carpets made in the region are much sought-after and rare indeed; and among them are some distinctive types. On narrow Dagestan rugs and runners, the main field is often divided into narrow diagonal strips of different colours. The strips may be decorated with botahs or with a curious little ornament consisting of a square with a hook-shaped 'head' and 'tail' emerging from diagonally opposite corners. This design is often combined with a Herati border of linked palmettes. The most harmonious colour combination is a brown, red and cream one which makes a pleasantly sombre impression.

opposite page
Seichur carpet. 19th century. Private collection, Milan

above
Karabagh 'Savonnerie' carpet

right
Dagestan prayer rug. Detail. Early 19th century

Another design has rows of step-sided diamonds, the 'steps' being a favourite Caucasian ornament. A rare type, made in a remote part of the Dagestan district, is the **Seichur** [76], which has two or more large medallions with diagonally extended arms like a St Andrew's cross. The decoration is more convincingly floral and less stylised than on most Caucasian carpets, and the predominant brown, blue and cream colour scheme is one of subtle harmony. The outer border usually contains 'running dog' pattern, sometimes so elaborate that it is hard to recognise.

Rarest of all but very beautiful are the prayer rugs of Dagestan. The early 19th-century example [77] is typical. The cream-yellow prayer niche fills almost the entire main field–so much so that it would be easy to overlook

its existence. The hypnotic effect of the grid or trellis is lightened by the asymmetrical scattering of pleasant, highly stylised little flowers and plants. The emphatic pattern in the main border is a highly stylised scroll.

Derbent is the chief city and market of Dagestan, situated in the northernmost part of the Caucasus, on the shores of the Caspian Sea. By contrast with other Dagestan carpets, on which the pile tends to be rather coarse, Derbent wares are notably thick and glossy. Otherwise production has been too eclectic to have any very individual characteristics; most of the Caucasian features such as eight-pointed stars, hooks, jagged edges and stepped lines appear, as do botahs and other Persian ornaments. The 19th-century carpet shown here [78], with its single, very narrow scroll border, its step-sided diamonds and triangles and crude little animal and bird figures, is effective by virtue of its dark blue ground and hard outlines. Modern Derbent carpets are normally very brightly coloured.

Chichi is the term used for rugs made by the Chechens, a Muslim people who still preserve

above
Chichi carpet. 19th century. Private collection, Milan

left
Derbent carpet. 19th century. Private collection, Milan

opposite, top
Sumak kilim carpet. Detail. See also title pages

opposite, below
Sumak carpet

below
Kuba Shirvan carpet

some nomad traditions, though drainage, agriculture and oil are having their inevitable effect on the way of life in the Chechen-Ingush Autonomous Republic. The Chechens were, incidentally, among the most devoted followers of Shamil, and thousands of them went into exile rather than accept Russian rule; during the Second World War they were suspected of being pro-German and were deported to Central Asia, allowed to return only in 1957.

The best Chichi rugs [78] are highly prized and are rarely seen outside the major collections. They are small, closely knotted and distinctive in design and colouring. They can be most certainly identified by their main border, which carries a series of diagonally placed lozenges or sticks, alternating with a stylised rosette or star, 'exploding' into separate pieces as in the illustration. The guards are decorated with the standard eight-pointed star and similar ornaments, set very close together, and the main field is equally tightly packed; the Chechen seems to have a positive aversion to unfilled spaces. The ornaments in the main field include repeated diamond-shapes, their outlines broken up into a series of hooks or key-pattern shapes, and rows of octagons; rosettes, stars, etc. in and around these ornaments fill the remaining spaces. But despite the crowded nature of their designs, Chichi rugs are restful to the eye, thanks to the mellow darkish colour scheme of red-yellow-brown tones on a deep blue ground in both the main field and the border.

Shirvan [78] is a village in the extreme south-east of the Caucasus (Azerbaijan), below the mountains and only a few miles from Baku. (Baku is the greatest city in the whole of the Caucasus, but the importance of its oil wells and port facilities has long overshadowed its carpet-making tradition.) Shirvan carpets are in fact produced over a wide area that includes the town of **Kuba,** which probably gave its name to the so-called 'Kabistan' rugs; actually there is no such place as Kabistan, and nowadays the term simply describes the best

Shirvans. Cotton is grown in the Shirvan area, and even in quite old carpets the warp and weft may be made of it, rather than of wool as in most other parts of the Caucasus. The knotting is generally fine, and the pile is clipped short; from the technical point of view modern workmanship, as often happens, is actually superior to that of previous centuries. As regards design, Shirvan has proved so eclectic that any extended attempt to describe its carpets would turn into a catalogue. But the eclecticism implies no failure of quality: the whole range of Caucasian motifs—stars, rosettes, stylised figures and flowers—is used, as are Persian floral designs, botah patterns, etc. On prayer rugs the hand of Fatima, the comb and the ewer also appear. If there is a characteristic Shirvan pattern it is on the border, where chains or interlacing patterns derived from Kufic lettering are often found [78]; it is interesting to compare these with the borders on Oushak carpets.

Finally there is the **Sumak** carpet [79], named after Shemakha, a small town in the same area, though the type was until recent years made over much of the southern Caucasus. The Sumak is not a 'true' carpet but a development of the kilims, the woven pileless carpets described earlier (see page 13). But the technique employed makes the Sumak much tougher and more tightly woven. Basically, it has weft threads stretching across the loom, so that the ground-weave is exactly the same as for a pile carpet; but instead of knots, additional coloured weft threads are woven in, as with kilims. The standard technique is to loop the thread over four warp threads on the surface of the carpet, bring it behind two more threads, and so on. By contrast with kilims, the ends of the coloured threads are left hanging free out of the back, so that the Sumak is not reversible. The back is a thick shaggy mass of trailing wool which makes the carpet a particularly warm one; the arrangement is less fragile than it seems, thanks to the full-length invisible weft threads, which are hammered down hard on to the col-

oured yarns as on ordinary carpets. In the East, Sumaks are often used on tables and beds as well as on the floor.

These are very attractive carpets indeed. The commonest design has a number of large blue octagons, or other shapes, arranged on a madder-red field; the octagon patterns are usually elaborated within and without, and the whole range of Caucasian ornament is drawn on to fill up the field background. A distinctive feature is the outermost border, which almost always contains the familiar continuous scroll or hook ('running dog') pattern. Sumaks are made in almost all accepted sizes. The finest are reckoned to come from Kuba; the lower-quality wares are called Derbent-Sumaks. Two very similar kinds of pileless carpet are found in this part of the Caucasus: the **Verneh,** usually carrying a pattern of squares, and the **Sileh,** notable for its blue and white colour scheme and very large S-shapes in boxes completely dominating the design.

Central Asia and Afghanistan

Bukhara tent strip

Bukhara saddlebag

Central Asia is a vast area that stretches away (from a Western point of view) beyond the Caspian Sea—which is why it is sometimes called Transcaspia. It is also known as western Turkestan, after the Turkomans or Turkmenians, who have roamed over it for the last thousand years. The Turkomans share a similar way of life and speak closely similar (Turkic) languages; other branches of this people crossed into the Caucasus and on to Anatolia—with such effect that it is now 'Turkey'. These connections tend to be overlooked in the West, but of course they are culturally important—and as late as the First World War there were Turkish leaders who dreamed of a great union of 'Turkish' peoples, stretching from Istanbul to the borders of China.

Central Asia is a land of great deserts sprinkled with oases, some of which gave birth to cities that became prosperous and powerful thanks to their roles as staging points on the caravan routes. It is also a land of steppes, until recent times fertile enough to support life but not to let it flourish: a land of hardy nomads, habituated to extremes of temperature and capable of surviving drought and famine—with the help of fairly frequent raids on the cities and settled areas.

Nomads and raiders the Turkomans remained through all the vicissitudes of their history. For a time they came under Mongol rule; later they had to acknowledge the suzerainty of Safavid Persia—the first time for two millennia that Persia had achieved any control in this part of the world. Finally, in the 1880s, the Turkomans, like the Caucasian peoples, fell victims to the great Russian drive into Asia—one of the lesser-known epics of the Age of Imperialism, and one of the few whose outcome has not been reversed. For the rest, Turkoman history consists of intertribal warfare and often remains obscure in its details; parts of this history must have influenced carpet design, since tribal symbols would inevitably have been affected by victories and defeats.

The craft and art of knotting probably originated among the Turkomans, and it is hardly possible to overestimate the part that carpets came to play in their lives. Carpets were one of the few forms of wealth that nomads—or rather nomad women—could create by their labour and carry with them on their travels; and they ranked as important items in the bride's dowry and the ceremonies surrounding the wedding celebrations. They were the chief sources of warmth and also of decoration inside the tent, so they were made not only as floor coverings but as hangings, decorative strips and entrance covers. And in lieu of tables, chairs and cupboards there were 'carpet' cushions scattered over the floor and 'carpet' bags holding the owner's possessions hanging from the roof. Prayer and funeral rugs, horse covers and camel rugs were also made of woven and knotted wool. The smaller items, being more often made simply for deco-

or styles. And since Turkoman rugs were made for use, and of very soft wool, only a few have survived from before the 19th century; of those that have, heavy wear and lack of documentation usually make it impossible to be anything like accurate in dating. However, that same remoteness of Central Asia ensured that the Turkoman way of life remained substantially untouched until remarkably late—even after the Russian Revolution—so that 19th- and early 20th-century examples have perfect integrity. For that matter, very good carpets with traditional designs are still produced in the manufactories of Ashkabad and other places in Soviet Central Asia, though carpet lovers feel they can never quite rival the older nomad work in warmth and spontaneity.

At first sight the various types of Turkoman carpet look very much alike. The differences are relatively subtle, and the increased appreciation of them in the last few decades probably owes something to the abstract art movement, which has developed the ability of people in the West to discriminate carefully among a variety of abstract patterns. There is no sense of drama in Turkoman designs, but instead a reflective repetition of unusually large geometric ornaments—the most important being the medallion-like tribal emblem, or gul [36], which is generally an octagon, square or elaborated diamond-shape. The colours are equally restrained, being dominated by very rich shades of red varying from a very dark brownish tone to one tinged with blue. Borders are usually the same ground colour as the main field, an almost ostentatious rejection of ostentation that is peculiar to Turkoman rugs.

As we have already noted, the smaller items are the most likely to be exceptions, and Turkoman bags have long been popular with Western collectors—though partly, it must be admitted,

Turkoman Bukhara rug

ration and display, are often brighter and more immediately pleasing than the larger.

However, **Turkoman** rugs are never very large. Almost all of them have been made for use by the tribe—which means within the confines of a tent; even in the 19th century, Central Asia was too remote to attract attention from European buyers, so consideration for the export market never influenced techniques

because Turkoman rugs are relatively hard to come by, since the actual number of this widely dispersed people is small. Some of the decorative hangings are mere strips, very narrow but as much as several yards long. On these the principle of repetition is abandoned, and all sorts of interesting little patterns appear for a few inches and then give way to new ones. Obviously such strips must have a special status –perhaps even a low one– which does not make a regular all-over design mandatory; possibly the nomad thought of them as equivalents to doodles.

The curtains which used to seal the tent entrance usually carry the hatchlu design [81]. This is one Turkoman design that can be identified without any difficulty, consisting of a broad cross, with arms of equal length, extending over the whole central field, which is thus divided into four compartments

of equal size. The hatchlu also appears on prayer rugs, and on these the vertical strut is sometimes broken into two niche-like objects; if not, there is a niche in the upper border on the narrow end of the rug. The presence of these borders at the top and/or bottom of the rugs is, incidentally, one of the peculiar features of Turkoman work. Hatchlus have no other special features, the decorative detail varying from tribe to tribe in line with the particular traditions of each one.

Technically, Turkoman workmanship is of surprisingly high quality. Most nomad rugs are largely and loosely knotted, with the pile left long; Turkoman rugs are tightly woven and finely knotted, and the pile is clipped very close. The wool is soft and lustrous, and the knots used are almost always Persian. In a good many examples the weave is made of goat-hair. Silk is rarely

found except on bridal rugs, but cotton is used quite often for the white areas in the design; it is of a purer and colder colour than wool, creating extreme contrasts that can be strident but tend to work well in the exclusively geometric designs of Turkoman rugs.

Good Central Asian carpets tend to be called **Bukharas** because the city used to be the assembly point and market for most of them; and, perhaps, because the very word 'Bukhara' –like 'Samarkand'– has a magi-

cal romantic quality that makes it the kind of trade name that advertisers dream about. In fact, carpets have never been made in Bukhara, which owed its commercial eminence to the lush oasis in which it grew up, making it the capital of one of the great Tartar emirates that replaced the Mongol Empire. In modern times the city's importance as a centre for the carpet trade has declined sharply with the rise of Ashkabad and the development of efficient long distance communications.

With more accurate study of Turkoman carpets it has become usual to classify them according to the tribe or area in which they were made–though most of the time the word 'Bukhara' is still tacked on. So the best Central Asian rugs are sometimes just **Tekes,** but more often 'Teke-Bukharas' [82]; the very finest of these are called–adding extravagance to injury–**'Royal Bukharas'.** The Teke live in an area stretching roughly from Ashkabad to Merv, along the Persian and Afghan frontiers. A deep red ground colour is characteristic, and the main pattern is the repeated Teke gul, octagonal in general outline but with small turns and curves that actually make it twenty-four sided. Both the shape and the decoration are of course always the same, since the gul is the tribal emblem; the decoration is in fact reminiscent of a heraldic design despite its abstract nature. A grid of vertical and horizontal lines covers the main field, neatly quartering all the guls. The illustration – of a classic 'Teke-Bukhara' – brings out the importance to the design of the alternating colours of the grounds within the guls, which is also a characteristic feature of Tekes. Between the guls are repeated star-shaped ornaments; the ones shown here are particularly spiky. The main borders carry large compartmented octagons, stars or similar shapes – not always, however, as large as the guls.

The Yomuds live further north, between the Teke and the Aral Sea. **Yomud** rugs [83] are almost as well thought of as those produced by the Teke. The ground red of 'Yomud-Bukharas' has a more brownish tone, and technically the rugs are not quite so fine, but they often have an intricacy and suggestion of fantasy that is very pleasing. The Yomud gul is a rough diamond-shape, much elaborated. The additional borders on the narrow ends often carry rows of little figures, so stylised that they have been variously interpreted. Of the other tribes, each with its own gul, the most important are the Salor, the Saryk and the Ersari. However, except among real specialists, Central Asian rugs made by any nomads but the Teke and Yomud are associated mainly with certain places.

Several different types of carpet are associated with **Khiva.** Not surprisingly, given its position just south of the Aral Sea, there is often a resemblance to Yomud work. **Pendeh,** much further south, is another centre at which rugs in various styles appear [83]. The best-known are **Kisil-Ayak,** which means 'golden-footed' and presumably describes the bright band often found at the foot of prayer rugs made in the area. The use of white cotton knots is particularly noticeable in Kisil-Ayaks.

Most 'Bukhara' rugs were made hundreds of miles from the city. Perversely, rugs from the one centre that is relatively close – the village of **Beshir** on the Amu Darya River – are not called Bukharas but are named from the village itself. Beshirs [84] are also unusual in not bearing the repeated-gul pattern, but instead a very wide variety of designs,

Beshir carpet. 19th century. Private collection, Milan

including a version of the Persian Herati. The Chinese cloud band is also found. A vestige of the gul remains in the octagons occasionally placed in the main field; in the 19th-century example illustrated here the octagons are noticeably unalike in both size and decoration. The dense hard-edged decoration is highly original, making an interesting contrast with the fascinatingly varied 'tree' design of the main border. The predominantly red and blue colour scheme is the conventional Turkoman one, but here and elsewhere it is easy to overlook the fact that the ground is dark blue; the density of the

decoration tends to deceive the eye into believing that the ground is red.

Closely related to Turkoman rugs are **Afghan** carpets [85], made by tribes of very similar stock; they are still weaving carpets, but now mainly as settled village dwellers instead of nomads. Afghan carpets have been known in the West for a long time – much better known than Central Asian rugs, for evident geographical reasons. Their restrained colours and decorative schemes appealed to the 19th-century gentleman's taste, and Afghans became standard equipment for the study and private library. Once more a deep red tone predominates, with decoration in dark blue and very sparingly used white, green or

Afghan carpet from Turkestan. Detail. 19th century. Private collection, Milan

Baluchi prayer rug

orange. The invariable design is one of rows of large squarish octagons, aptly nicknamed 'elephants' feet'. The inside of each octagon is usually divided into four compartments with alternately coloured grounds, as on Teke rugs. The border may consist of many strips, sometimes of a surprising decorative complexity that is easy to overlook because concealed by the ground colour.

Because of their early involvement with the export market, Afghan carpets come in most sizes. 19th-century examples may be finely knotted and clipped short; however, on those made for use among the mountains and snows of the Hindu Kush the pile is left long for protection against the cold. Later Afghans are generally only of medium density, but the wool is almost always of good quality, with a pleasant sheen, and worked with Persian knots. The ground-weave is frequently of goat-hair instead of sheep's wool. Although found far less often in Central Asia, prayer rugs with mihrabs or the hatchlu design were also made

by the Afghans.

No reader should now be surprised to learn that **Baluchi** rugs [85] are not produced in Baluchistan, which is the name of a province of Pakistan and also the area of Persia just across the frontier. They are made much further north, in the Persian province of Khorassan and just over the Russo-Persian border; in fact the best-quality Baluchi rugs are known as Meshed Baluchis, after the chief town of Khorassan. Being nomad work, they are generally quite small. The ground-weave was always made of wool until recent years, when cotton began to be used instead. The knots are Persian.

Although the dominating presence of red and blue, and the almost exclusively geometric decoration, are typical of the Turkoman group to which these rugs belong, the range of designs on Baluchi rugs is unusually wide, no doubt as a result of Persian influence. Even the sophisticated botah pattern appears on some examples. Grounds may be camel-coloured, especially for the

mihrabs on prayer rugs, which are perhaps the most interesting of Baluchi wares; the effect is achieved simply by using natural camel-hair. On these rugs the mihrab is a straightforward rectangular object (by contrast with the rounded, pointed and fancy-topped structures seen in other carpet regions), though the decoration both inside and outside it may be very elaborate; the most common is the Tree of Life in a very rigid stylised form, the branches sticking out from the trunk almost at an angle of ninety degrees. In the example here [85], the branches actually are at right angles and have been extended to meet the sides of the mihrab in a grid pattern set against a camel-hair ground. Such designs are helpful in understanding how representational scenes, figures and objects can be distorted or transformed into abstracts: the mere process of decorative elaboration—extending lines, arranging roughly similar features into patterns—has almost caused the tree to disappear.

China and Chinese Turkestan

Chinese (or Eastern) Turkestan lies several hundred miles east of the main Turkoman territory, in what is now the Chinese province of Sinkiang. This land is even more inhospitable than Central Asia. Much of it is fiery desert, too hot and dry for even the intrepid caravans crossing Asia by the Silk Route. They bypassed the desert, travelling south through the oases at Yarkand and Kashgar before emerging at Khotan; which is why these three towns grew up—and became the main carpet centres for the whole region.

The techniques of weaving and knotting must have been known in this part of the world since very early times. A few fragments of pile carpet, found at Turfan in the north-east of the province, survive from the 5th or 6th century AD; and of course Pazyryk is not very far away—in terms of Asian distances—just over the northernmost frontier in the Soviet Union.

The history of Chinese Turkestan is one of great migrations and invasions—by the Turkomans, who still form the bulk of the nomad population, as well as by the all-conquering Mongols and other peoples. Intermittently over many centuries the Chinese exercised some sort of control in this region, and the resulting fusion of Turkoman and Chinese styles gives these **Samarkand** carpets [86, 87] much of their special interest.

They are universally called Samarkands despite the fact that that glamorous city lies some two hundred miles west of Sinkiang, in the Uzbek SSR. In this instance the explanation is that Samarkand served as the main 19th-century market for carpets from Chinese Turkestan, which had no commercial outlets to speak of in central and eastern China.

Technically speaking, Samarkand carpets are not of high quality. The wool is rather loosely spun and the knot-density is generally low, in striking contrast to Turkoman work in Central Asia. On the other hand the wool is so constituted that the colours show up particularly brightly—and the special charm of Samarkand carpets lies in their pleasant colours and designs. Despite the subtle virtues of Central Asian rugs, it comes as something of a relief to look at bold varied uncluttered designs in light bright colours—yellow, light blue, mauve and orange as well as the familiar red and grey.

In all the Samarkand designs the rigid lines of Turkoman geometry tend to be softened by Chinese and even some Persian influence, which are also responsible for the inclusion of floral and symbolic elements. Many of the rugs carry one, two or three medallions with gentle outlines, often containing one or another version of the several highly stylised cloud forms developed by the Chinese; they seem to have been particularly congenial to the carpet-makers of this region, who frequently elaborated them into all-over lattice or scroll designs.

below
Modern Chinese rug with a dragon design

above
Samarkand carpet from Mongolia. 18th century. Private collection, Milan

opposite, top
Samarkand carpet from Sinkiang

opposite, below
Turkoman Samarkand carpet. 19th century

Vase and tendril patterns, Trees of Life and other motifs are also found, but the most notable pattern is undoubtedly a pomegranate-tree, shown growing from a small vase and spreading its branches over the whole main field. The example illustrated here [86], with its pink fruits and dark blue ground, is both splendid and typical. The border of stylised flowers is effective but unusual, as most Samarkands carry variations of the key-T-running-dog group of patterns, sometimes with the addition of a wider band of rosettes.

The craft of knotting seems to have entered China from Eastern Turkestan along the Silk Route, and to have remained substantially confined to the north and north-west of the country, within reasonable distance from Peking and the imperial court. Given the climate and the early Chinese adoption of tables, chairs and cupboards, carpets had no functional qualities important enough to offset their cost; so they remained essentially display items, mainly produced for the Emperor, his courtiers and high civil servants. The earliest surviv-

ing examples date from the Ming dynasty (1368–1644). No one can say whether or not the carpet was known before Ming times; it is not impossible, since the wool used by the Chinese is so delicate that their carpets age and even fall to pieces within a surprisingly short time. But literary sources, which are eloquent in praise of textiles, appliqué work, etc., are suspiciously silent on the subject of knotted carpets, so they may well have been quite late arrivals in China.

The Chinese have never ranked carpet-making high in the list of their arts, and Western experts have followed suit—though for long periods over the past century the general public has rushed to buy debased 'Chinese-style' carpets made for export in China itself, Hong Kong, Japan and even Smyrna! Genuine Chinese carpets have probably been underestimated, partly because of their technical limitations and partly because they violate purist notions of what a carpet should be and look like. For example, the Chinese habit of clipping round the decorations, so that they stand out in relief, offends against the functional quality that carpets are supposed to possess, and is at first visually disconcerting. But whether the objection represents purity or prejudice must remain a matter of opinion.

The colour scheme too is unlike that of most other carpets, with its pastel shades of blue, yellow and pink. Even medallion carpets, which had become common by the time of the Ch'ien Lung reign (1735–99), have distinctive Chinese delicacy. Some examples even achieve the swift, summary look of Chinese paintings—the 18th-century saddle cover [88] for instance. This comes from Tibet but was probably imported from China; there is certainly no evidence that carpets were actually made in Tibet. On this piece the blossoms in the two medallions have a cursory spontaneous quality that might have been created with a few strokes of a master's ink-loaded brush. Their fragility is emphasised by the restful ground colour and set off by the bold simple border.

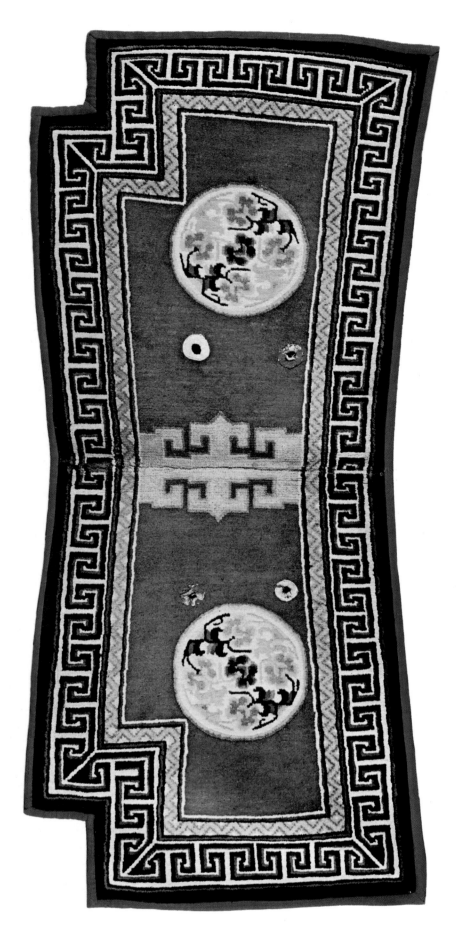

Tibetan saddle cover. 18th century

Chinese carpets are as hard to 'place' as they are to date. As with other Chinese arts, regional variations are remarkably small: hammered into a single nation in the 3rd century BC, China has maintained a cultural unity that mirrors its political unity. This is clearest of all in the symbolism of Chinese carpets, which derives from several sources and yet is entirely homogeneous. Confucianism, Taoism and Buddhism all contributed symbols to Chinese art and thought. But though most Chinese believed in one of these systems and disbelieved in the other two, they happily took over the symbols of all three. These were treated as forming a common stock which could be drawn on in any desirable permutations. Yet the individual symbols lost none of their force, though meanings and allusions did tend to multiply over the centuries. The Chinese mind seems to be uniquely symbol-prone, with the result that neither the meaning nor the visual expression of the symbol ever disappears entirely through stylisation or distortion – a fact that sets the Chinese carpet apart from almost all others.

It is worth noticing a few of the most common symbols on Chinese carpets – a few only, since an exhaustive description would make a lengthy book on its own. The best-known of all – thanks to the revived Western belief in the mysterious East as a source of wisdom – is the yin-yang symbol [89]; its swastika-circle form graphically conveys the endless alternation and interaction of dark/female/earth (yin) and light/male/heaven (yang). The dragon and phoenix represent virtually the same pairing, but in addition the dragon – with five toes – stands for the emperor, while the phoenix stands for the empress. Other dragons, variously equipped, are of mythical rather than symbolic significance. The *fo* is a Buddhist symbol, protective against evil: a lion, often also called a dog, since in some renderings he bears a distinct resemblance to a pekinese and is shown playing with a ball. The various cloud patterns symbolise heaven and the protection of heaven; hence, appropriately,

they usually surround other figures or symbols on the carpet. In effect such symbols are good luck wishes or charms. Stags, cranes and pines signify old age, regarded by all Chinese in times past as a reward for right living. Lotus, peony, plum and chrysanthemum represent the four seasons. And there are a great variety of symbols based on the ennumerations dear to the Chinese heart—the Eight Immortals, the Eight Precious Things, the Hundred Antiquities, and so on. It follows that the majority of old Chinese carpets, however artistically designed, are lengthy messages from the donor to the recipient or from the owner to the gods. However, it is true that most of them amount to no more than a series of wishes for the kind of good fortune every Chinese desired: good luck and

the protection of heaven, many sons, long life and an easy death. *Fu* and *shou*—conventionalised Chinese characters standing for good luck and long life—may also appear on carpets.

The pseudo-Chinese carpet has now disappeared (at least from China itself), but so to all intents and purposes have the traditional designs. Modern Chinese carpets are made after the classic French floral designs, and Chinese 'Savonneries' and 'Aubussons' [89] are exported in large numbers. They are mass-produced in state factories, and although they are hand-knotted they have the finish of machine-made products. Inevitably, connoisseurs do not like them, but in a world of rocketing prices it can hardly be denied that they provide an answer to a genuine demand.

above
Chinese 'Aubusson' carpet made in Tientsin

above left
Chinese carpet. 19th century. Private collection, Milan

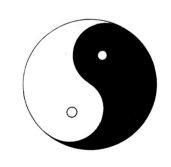

Yin-yang symbol

India and Pakistan

Indian prayer rug. Late 17th century. Österreichisches Museum für Angwandte Kunst, Vienna

Carpets were even less functional objects in India than they were in China, and virtually everything that has survived from past centuries bears the hallmark of a court art. Production on any scale–and perhaps production of any sort–dates from the **Mogul** period, which begins with the conquest of northern India by Babur in the late 1520s. The Moguls, descended from Tamerlane (Mogul=Mongol), had entered India from the northwest and were thoroughly Persianised in culture. They made Persian the language of their court, introduced the Persian art of the miniature to India, and imported Persian workmen to weave their carpets. Workshops developed round the imperial cities of Agra, Fathpur and Lahore, and under Akbar the Great (1556–1605) and his successors, splendid Indian versions of the classic floral [90], garden and hunting carpets were produced. The silk carpets made in India are even reported to have surpassed their Persian originals. In the 17th century a native Indian style began to develop, notably in floral designs treated with much greater naturalism than their Persian equivalents [91]. The scenes on Indian hunting carpets [92] are treated differently too. They are less static; men and beasts–real and mythical–fight, run and rear convincingly, seemingly more involved in the action than they are in Persian carpets. Interestingly enough, exactly the same difference exists between Persian and Indian miniatures.

The decline of the Moguls and the impact of European demand had a predictably disastrous effect on carpet-making. Modern India is again marketing Savonneries and other carpets, but the success story of recent years has been the boom in Pakistan. As in China, carpet-making in Pakistan has been organised on an impressive industrial scale, underpinned by massive government subsidies. Pakistani carpets too are mass-produced–but mass-produced by hand, with hundreds of looms assembled on one site. Furthermore, Pakistani carpets are finely knotted and in all other respects so efficiently produced that they can be mistaken for machine-made objects–which is, of course, one of the criticisms levelled at them. **'Pakistan Bukharas'** [91] were the first well-known line, but the factories soon turned to imitating Persian and Caucasian carpets too. Apart from the aesthetic objections to imitation, Pakistani carpets are not true copies because they are made without the defects and irregularities of the originals. They are also standardised in knotting, depth of pile, etc., making no allowance for the regional and tribal variations that give Persian, Caucasian and Central Asian carpets much of their appeal. Still, it would not be reasonable to expect too much of mass-produced goods–and how infuriated connoisseurs would be if there *were* such a thing as a perfect imitation! The great virtue of the Pakistani carpet is, of course, that it costs about a quarter of the

left
Indian 'Aubusson' carpet of the 20th century, from Kashmir. Private collection, Milan

price of a Persian work it imitates; and it is likely to become relatively cheaper still in the next few years.

above
Pakistan Bukhara

Mogul carpet. 17th century

Mogul hunting carpet. 16th or early
17th century. Museum of Fine Arts,
Boston (Gift of Mrs Frederick L.
Ames, in the name of Frederick L.
Ames)

Collecting, Caring and Repairing

Collecting

No book—let alone a short general one like this—can provide a substitute for years of experience. The committed collector reads everything he can find on the subject and also haunts the museums and dealers' premises; and even so he may make serious mistakes in this tricky field. It is true that deliberate fakes are less common in the carpet trade than in most other crafts and arts, though they are by no means unknown. But, as the foregoing chapters should have made clear, there are a multitude of imitations, variations and revivals at all levels of skill and seriousness—from the Mogul and Turkish tributes to Persian genius, which are themselves old and valuable, to the Pakistani Bukhara, Smyrna Chinese and Chinese Savonnerie. Collecting is complicated still further by the lack of stable technical criteria, utterly bewildering to anyone but the specialist: it is not always the finest knotting, shortest pile or glossiest wool that command the highest price and reputation; and even age and beauty of design need not be decisive factors. Prices are almost a separate study, determined by supply and demand but more difficult than ever to keep track of in the Age of Inflation. In these circumstances, intelligent buying is hard enough for the expert or dedicated collector: for the ordinary man who has read a book and wants to buy a carpet, it is a near-impossibility.

There is, of course, only one answer: to find a reputable and patient dealer and put great reliance on his guidance. Every book on carpets repeats this same piece of advice; but, all the same, every year the readers of such books cannot resist the lure of seemingly fabulous discounts or the low prices sometimes encountered at auctions. Naturally such attempts to secure bargains without adequate knowledge invite a disaster, and one usually entailing far greater loss than the hoped-for saving—quite apart from the disappointment of owning a damaged or worthless object in place of a useful pleas-

Part of a warehouse showing fine carpets from central and north-western Persia, with Tabriz in the foreground

Repairing a carpet

trast, an all-over pattern will not be spoiled by the presence of furniture, and may even benefit by having its all-too-regular pattern interrupted. The height and length of the room must also be considered, and so must the amount and quality of the light. For those who cannot build houses to suit their carpets, such apparent trivialities are of decisive importance.

'Buyer, beware!' is no longer the rule–not, at any rate, if you do business with our reputable dealer. If you change your mind within a reasonable time you can normally trade in the carpet you have bought in exchange for one of similar price. And if you discover a defect in the carpet after you have bought it, the firm will take it back; with objects that have been transported thousands of miles, accidents can happen that remain unobserved by the most conscientious dealer. Still, it is better to avoid disappointment and inconvenience by trying to make sure that the carpet is in good condition before you write out a cheque and arrange for its delivery.

This is something the ordinary buyer can do for himself with a reasonable certainty of success, provided he has the self-confidence to spend time on the premises making a thorough scrutiny. He must look all over the surface for traces of wear, damage or moth, check that the edges are not ragged, and then turn the carpet over and examine the back with at least as much care. For it is on the back that repairs and concealed joins will show; and worn patches on the back are in some respects more serious than on the front, since they will have loosened or severed the knots, making the pile liable just to fall out at any time. Any other peculiar features, such as harsher colouring on the back than on the pile, should be queried, since they may indicate that the carpet is a relatively recent one that has been treated (for example by chemical washing) to look much older than it is. Finally, the carpet should be folded over with the pile on the inside, and then pulled over a little more, firmly but gently. If there is a noise of

ing one. With a good dealer, on the other hand, you will not get a bargain, but you will get value for money–and the certainty of having got it. If such tame procedures lack the thrill of the chase it may be some consolation to reflect that the greatest of experts is not likely to find stupendous bargains, either in the local junk shop or the Eastern bazaar. For that matter, there are few art objects to be picked up cheaply any more; and carpets are too conspicuous and expensive to be among that few.

Your dealer must be patient and friendly as well as trustworthy. If he tries to rush you and make a quick sale he is not necessarily a shark (though such behaviour does and should arouse suspicion), but he is not much use to a client with a limited budget. No good carpet is so cheap that such a person can afford to buy it without guidance, and time to reflect.

There are some decisions a dealer cannot make for you: he provides the information on which a choice should be based, but cannot climb into your skin. Each person has his own idiosyncrasies and will prefer a particular style or type of carpet–though there is everything to be said for broadening and deepening one's taste by looking at as many good examples as possible. The carpet's suitability to its future surroundings will also be a consideration, and it is naturally up to the customer to see that he does not buy an extravagant floral rug for his monastically severe writing room, or an elephant's-feet Afghan for a pastel pink bedroom. To be more serious, the buyer must take into account the shape, function and furnishings of the room which is to be carpeted. For example, a medallion carpet will lose much of its impact if the room contains a good deal of furniture; the design is most effective if all its related parts can be seen. By con-

creaking or cracking the carpet has been rotted by damp and is irreparably damaged; it should only be bought on the understanding that it is defective and priced as such. In practice, such a purchase would only be made of a fine antique whose aesthetic qualities outweighed the fact that it was damaged; and since it would be destined for the wall rather than a floor, it would still have a reasonable expectation of life.

The care of carpets

If you buy a genuine Oriental carpet you know you have something that was made to last—but not necessarily to endure gross neglect, scuffing by shoes or pressure from heavy furniture. Loosely knotted all-wool carpets are the most vulnerable, but it is a good idea to know just what kind of carpets you own and what kind of treatment they can stand.

The main enemies of carpets are damp and dirt. Carpets can get wet without harm if they are properly dried out; if they are not, the damp rots the weave. So a damp carpet should always be thoroughly dried and aired, and carpets should never be laid on newly washed floors. For the same reason, the carpet surface should be washed with soap or a foam, using the minimum amount of water. Carpet beating is no longer necessary; everyday cleaning can be done with a vacuum cleaner, which should also sometimes be passed over the back of the rug; regular use of the vacuum cleaner is important because grit will otherwise work its way deep into the carpet and damage the knots. A well cared-for carpet should need deep-cleansing only at long intervals, and that is another job best left to professionals, who will test the colours for fastness and take all other necessary precautions.

Felt underlay protects the backs of carpets and also keeps them from slipping on the floor. Felt can also be placed under heavy pieces of furniture to take off some of the pressure on the carpet. If possible, the furniture—or the carpet—should be moved fairly often to give the crushed pile a chance to spring back.

Repairing carpets

There is little to be said about repairing except that it is unthinkable to repair a quality carpet yourself: you must go to a specialist. Obviously, the earlier that wear or damage are detected, the easier it is to repair the carpet and the less the operation will cost. Once damaged, the carpet may disintegrate with surprising speed; if the edges in particular become worn, the pile itself will start to come away. A small repair which shows only on the back will not detract from the beauty or the value of a carpet. Properly looked after, your carpet should never require more attention than that, and should give a lifetime's service. If you are really careless or unlucky, the repairer may still be able to save your carpet, but it will be a very expensive operation and may simply not be worth it.

Antique carpets are another matter, since it is very difficult indeed to match the wool. The repair must be done with wool of the same quality, dyed the same shade and at about the same time as the damaged piece, so that the colour will have faded to exactly the same extent. To put it moderately, this is asking a great deal. And that is why even the most insensitive owners never dream of treading on their antique carpets! Of course, if the antique is artistically valuable enough, almost any effort and expense are justified, including the kind of cannibalism that was necessary to restore the Ardebil carpet.

This chapter provides no more than an outline and cannot adequately deal with a subject of such vital importance. It is worth repeating that the would-be collector should take the best available advice on every aspect of carpet buying, maintenance and repair. It is hardly possible to be too cautious or too thorough in these matters.

Collecting tomorrow

Finally, what of future prospects for the collector? Frankly, the outlook is bleak—particularly for Persian carpets, which are, when all is said and done, the aristocrats of the East. Carpet-making in Persia is still essentially a domestic or small-scale local industry, and with every year it becomes more of an anomaly in the emerging pattern of Persian life. This oil-rich country is now industrialising at some speed, with the result that there are thousands of new jobs being created in the towns which attract poorly paid rural labour. Carpet-making is particularly vulnerable since, as we have seen, the amount of time and labour invested in a single carpet is enormous, and could only be properly recompensed by a very high sale price. Nowadays child labour has been prohibited, and its illegal continuation is becoming less common, however remote the region. Even the Oriental woman now expects decent wages if she remains at the loom.

The result, from the point of view of the Western buyer, is tragic: production has fallen off, prices have risen and, inevitably, Western demand has slackened. It is this situation which has made possible the production of still more 'Persian' carpets in Pakistan and even in countries such as Romania, where labour costs are still low. It has also brought the indigenous products of North Africa and Egypt on to the export market, though these are mats rather than carpets.

All this is only to say that the bonanza years, based on the exploitation of cheap labour, are over; and a good thing too. Predictions are always dangerous, but it does seem highly unlikely that the trend will be reversed; instead, some day even Pakistan and India will go the same way. And, unfortunately, as far as carpets are concerned this means that the good hand-knotted piece is going to become a luxury item. It is still possible to acquire Oriental carpets without being wealthy—but it would be as well to start in the very near future.

Acknowledgments

The illustrations on pages 17, 21, 37, 38 top, 53 top left, 55 top, 74 top, 78 bottom, 79 top, 80 top, 80 bottom, 81 bottom, 86 top, 87 bottom, 91 bottom left, 93 and 94 and on the endpapers were photographed at L. Kelaty Ltd, London, by courtesy of Mr Sion Mehdi, and those on pages 33 bottom, 53 bottom left, 55 bottom, 70 top, 70 bottom, 73 right and 79 bottom at the Vigo-Sternberg Galleries, London, by courtesy of Mr Charles Sternberg.

Photographs
British Library, London 23; Colorific–Carl Purcell, London 15; Cooper-Bridgeman Library, London 54 left; Dominique Darbois, Paris 22, 24 left, 45 right, 66 bottom, 67 right, 73 left; Fratelli Fabbri Editori, Milan 12 bottom, 24 right, 26, 43 top, 43 bottom, 47 bottom, 48 left, 48 right, 50 bottom, 52 top, 52 bottom, 56, 58, 59, 61 bottom, 65 top, 66 top, 67 left, 68 top, 68 bottom, 72, 75 bottom, 76, 78 top left, 78 top right, 81 top, 83 left, 84, 85 left, 87 top, 89 left, 91 top left; Olga Ford, Leicester 6; P. B. Gotch 20; Hamlyn Group–Paul Forrester 17, 21, 37, 38 top, 53 top left, 55 top, 74 top, 78 bottom, 79 top, 80 top, 80 bottom, 81 bottom, 86 top, 87 bottom, 91 bottom left, 93, 94, endpapers; Hamlyn Group Picture Library 13, 19, 28, 35, 41, 45 left, 49, 51 right, 60, 63, 75 left, 77 bottom, 82, 83 right, 86 bottom, 88; Metropolitan Museum of Art, New York 69 bottom; Arnoldo Mondadori Editore, Milan 14 top left, 14 top right, 40, 42, 46, 47 top, 50 top, 54 right, 56–57, 77 top, 85 right, 89 right; Museum of Fine Arts, Boston, Massachusetts 92; National Gallery, London 31, 61 top; Österreichisches Museum für Angewandte Kunst, Vienna 62, 90; Pictor International, London 7; Scala, Antella 27, 33 top; Sotheby Parke Bernet & Co, London 25, 30, 44, 51 left, 53 right, 57, 64, 65 bottom, 69 top, 71, 74 bottom, 91 right; Victoria and Albert Museum, London 29, 32; ZEFA–Hans Schmied 11; ZEFA–I. Steinhoff 9 bottom; ZEFA–Vigo-Sternberg 33 bottom, 53 bottom left, 55 bottom, 70 top, 70 bottom, 73 right, 79 bottom; ZEFA–R. Waldkirch 8, 9 top, 14 bottom; ZEFA–H. Wiesner 10.